PRACTICAL SOCIAL WORK
Series Editor: Jo Campling

BASW

Editorial Advisory Board:
Terry Bamford, Malcolm Payne, Peter Riches
and Sue Walrond-Skinner

Social work is at an important stage in its development. All professions must be responsive to changing social and economic conditions if they are to meet the needs of those they serve. This series focuses on sound practice and the specific contribution which social workers can make to the well-being of our society in the 1980s.

The British Association of Social Workers has always been conscious of its role in setting guidelines for practice and in seeking to raise professional standards. The conception of the Practical Social Work series arose from a survey of BASW members to discover where they, the practitioners in social work, felt there was the most need for new literature. The response was overwhelming and enthusiastic, and the result is a carefully planned, coherent series of books. The emphasis is firmly on practice, set in a theoretical framework. The books will inform, stimulate and promote discussion, thus adding to the further development of skills and high professional standards. All the authors are practitioners and teachers of social work representing a wide variety of experience.

JO CAMPLING

PRACTICAL SOCIAL WORK

BASW

Computers in Social Work

Bryan Glastonbury

MACMILLAN

First published 1985

Published by
Higher and Further Education Division
MACMILLAN PUBLISHERS LTD
Houndmills, Basingstoke, Hampshire RG21 2XS
and London
Companies and representatives
throughout the world

Filmsetting by Vantage Photosetting Co Ltd,
Eastleigh and London
Printed in Hong Kong

British Library Cataloguing in Publication Data
Glastonbury, Bryan
Computers in social work.
1. Public welfare—Great Britain—Data
processing
I. Title
361'.941'02854   HV245
ISBN 0–333–37670–6
ISBN 0–333–37671–4   Pbk

Contents

Preface

Computers have been used in the personal social services for over a decade now. Most social services departments use them, as do many probation services and larger voluntary organisations. Yet they have not impinged much on the daily activities of social workers, perhaps because they have been seen as tools of management, or perhaps because it has been assumed that bringing practitioners and computers together would be a recipe for upheaval. After all, computers are more than just pieces of equipment – they represent highly charged controversies.

The decision to write this book reflects the observation, which must be clear to all of us, that computers are moving fast into many aspects of our lives – into offices, schools, homes and the contacts we have with 'officialdom'. The computer seems unstoppable, and is already starting to wind its way into professional social work. We cannot, and indeed may not, want to bring it to a halt, so instead we need to understand it and put it to sensible use. Computing can be studied as a separate subject, to be kept at arm's length by all but the enthusiasts and those who cannot avoid it. That may be a viable approach to computer *science*, but it will not serve for computer *application*, and it has proved challenging to have the invitation from Macmillan and the British Association of Social Workers to write about computers in a series on social work practice.

I am grateful to several colleagues from the Department of Social Work Studies at Southampton University, and to many staff of government and local authority services for help in gathering material. Mike Gardner from Hampshire Social Services Department and Allan D. Maclean of the Home Office

Research and Planning Unit have been especially helpful. However, three people have made major contributions. Charles Whaley, from Cornwall Social Services Department, gave me a flying start by letting me have a copy of his study of computers in a local social services office (done as part of a post-qualifying course at Plymouth Polytechnic), and with it an extensive bibliography. David Ward, from Hampshire Social Services Department, gave me time and documents for the case-study of Hampshire's computer system, and later made valuable comments on the draft of Chapter 3. Sheena Kimberley talked to many social workers about their attitudes to and experiences of computers, and has also been a dependable 'second opinion' on the script.

I have tried to present a balanced view of the issues surrounding the use of computers in the personal social services, but I should be counted as a computer buff, who believes firmly in the creative potential of the new technology within social work practice.

Southampton   BRYAN GLASTONBURY
1985

Introduction

Can computers do social work? This is as pertinent a question now as it was over a decade ago when it was first posed as the title of an article in a social work journal (Abels, 1972). The fantasy should not be taken too far into the realms of science fiction, to portray a vision of redundant social workers, and area offices full of TV screens. Rather it is a practical question – what can computers do to help in running social work agencies and providing services for customers?

The purpose of this book is to answer such a question, and many others which inevitably arise from it. As a society and a work force we are right in the middle of a massive technological metamorphosis. The young people coming up through schools and universities are the first generation educated, however skimpily, for the computer age. Today's social workers, even the young ones, come from the tail end of an era when a file is located inside a manila folder, not in a data-base. Leaving aside the vital question of how far the transition will go, it is likely that any move towards new technology in social work will be uncomfortable. It will involve new learning; it will continue to raise political and ethical dilemmas; and the change itself will create more work, especially during the years when old and new systems run side by side.

Much of the handling of computing has been designed or had the effect of making adults feel inferior. On TV advertisements smug 'Acorn'-fed children look indulgently at their stone-age parents; the newspapers bombard us with reviews of the continual flow of new systems; and the magazines show that computing would win any prize for the speediest development of the most obscure and jargon-filled specialist language. Therefore any book which wants to convince social workers that computers are not to be feared, and do indeed have some utility, must begin with some simple explanations and removal of mystique. This is the purpose of Chapter 1.

The chapter offers answers to some basic questions – What is a computer? What can it do? What is the difference between the machine hidden in the bowels of County Hall and the small keyboard plugged into the TV at home? Where do word-processors fit in? Are computers just for numbers, or can they really handle words and concepts? Can they think? Do they have a will of their own? What sort of jobs are they capable of doing which might be of any practical use to a social worker? Among all the jargon, what are the terms that it could be useful to understand? Is it easy to use a computer without making it do something disastrous? What does a social worker need to know so as to avoid being confused or upstaged at meetings?

This first chapter also tries to describe with precision just what we generally assume to be encompassed when we use the umbrella term 'computer'. Strictly speaking the computer itself is a relatively small part of the range of equipment. Most of the bits (called 'peripherals') have to do with communicating in some form or other with the computer – the keyboard, screen, printer and so forth. Furthermore, much of our image of this scene, whether of banks of flickering lights and whizzing spools from TV films (totally obsolete from the technological point of view since the 1960s!), or of vast stores of confidential and invasive personal information, or of 'personalised' advertising letters and bills for 0 pence, is only partly to do with computing. It is as much connected with the development of telecommunications, which allows us to pass and receive messages at very high speed over great distances, and move around enormous chunks of information at the pressing of a few buttons. On their own, computers would have made much less impact if their technological development had not paralleled similar advances in ways of communicating.

Chapter 1 will have a slant towards social work, but is mainly concerned to offer a more general introduction to computing. Those who are already well into computing can pass over it, just as they can skip the early part of Chapter 2. This chapter starts with a brief history of computing, partly to explain why it is so often referred to as 'the new technology', and partly as a feeder into a discussion of the gradual intrusion of computers into the personal social services. One of the conclusions to be drawn from a historical review is that almost all the pioneering efforts, and the bulk of current use, is in service management rather than front-line practice. Social workers themselves, whether from lack of opportunity or motivation, have tended to keep a distance, and retain a commitment to traditional ways of working. In the broader context of computer applications this places social workers firmly in the rearguard, though their colleagues in America have been more adventurous. The chapter will not go into any detail about technical developments, but it will advance the argument that in most sectors of the economy computer capability continues well ahead of actual use. Specifically in the personal social services it is no longer relevant to talk of computer possibilities as 'on the horizon' or 'just around the corner'. A recent survey by the Local Authority Management Services and Computer Committee's Social Services Applications Group (LAMSAC, 1982) suggests that most, maybe all, social services departments now have access to computers. Probation services are moving in the same direction. But access is one matter, use is another. Few if any of these agencies will be using more than a part, sometimes a small portion, of the range of useful tasks the computer could undertake.

The chapter also suggests that the development of computing in social services departments has been somewhat opportunistic, without testing feasibility in a careful and thorough way. It is arguable that there is a rather wider range of issues worthy of consideration than is generally acknowledged, and that these can be structured into a coherent sequence of decisions to be taken in relation both to determining whether a computer is needed and going through the process of installation.

Chapters 3 and 4 look in more detail at what is happening in the agencies, both with routine computer work and some of the pioneering and developmental activities. Chapter 3 is a case-study offering a detailed narrative of a decade of computing in one social services department. Hampshire has one of the largest departments in the country. It has also been using computers longer than most – since 1974 – and has invested in a large and continually growing management information system. More recently the Department has started to involve front-line staff, both in computer usage and programme development. Hampshire is not offered as a case-study because it is 'typical' or because it is the most advanced, but rather for the continuity and extent of planning which has gone into the system, and the way all the anticipated dilemmas and controversies have, at some stage in the last decade, come to the surface.

Hampshire's arrangements are called a Management Information System – appropriate in the early years, but less so following recent developments. On a wider stage the concept of the Management Information System (MIS) has faced many critics – one commentator sub-titled a book on computers in welfare 'The MIS-match' (Dery, 1981). Some of the criticism has focused on the flaws and inadequacies of such systems; some has been motivated by the feeling that there is little of value in all of this for the practising social worker. Chapter 4 does not argue this issue (later chapters take it up), but instead offers some of the raw material which will help the reader decide if computers can and do have a useful role in practice. The chapter will look at a variety of computer applications in use among social workers, ranging from calling up central data stores for information about clients and resources, through programs for various forms of assessment (welfare benefits is the best-known one), to computer-aided decision-making and therapy. All of this is newer than the management systems mentioned earlier, and therefore tends to be experimental. In the context of computing 'experimental' is likely to mean unreliable, inaccurate and hedged with limitations, but it is important not to dismiss trial programs because they have prolonged teething troubles. A lengthy refining and correcting process (called 'de-bugging' in the jargon) is an integral part of computer programming. The point about the applications described in this chapter is that they are all in some form of use in practical settings. They are not in the realm of wishful thinking – or nightmare!

However important it may be for social workers to be understanding, appreciative and sympathetic about computing there remains the task of taking the plunge and becoming a 'hands-on' user. This is likely to mean either working with a desktop micro-computer or sitting at a terminal. There is little difference. The micro will be all together on the desk, either in a single container, or as an array of equipment connected by a tangle of cables. There may be a few 'setting up' activities before getting into action, but the micro is seen as a more immediately responsive piece of apparatus, more 'user-friendly'. A terminal is 'remote' in the sense that it connects to the computer proper at some distance, often in another building or place. There is no setting up because someone else is looking after the computer, and the opening task is 'keying in', which is equivalent to applying for and establishing the right to communicate.

Chapter 5 looks at what is involved in becoming a user. It is not a d-i-y guide (anyone who is going to work at a computer can expect an introductory course), but aims to tackle two major impediments to social workers moving easily into the role. One concerns the mystification surrounding computing, a theme which will already have been touched on in an earlier chapter. Indeed the concept features regularly in social work itself, so the term 'de-mystification' will be understood in its multiple nuances. There is an entertaining side to the strained efforts of a computer specialist and a social worker to talk to the other, each in his or her own jargon, but it is also a serious and harmful block. Should the social worker speak computerese? Is there scope for a common language? What are the similarities and differences in the mental processes of the two?

The second impediment derives from the fears many social workers have that in order to use computers they will have to undertake a whole new range of learning. There is a specific fear that this will require a high degree of numeracy. This chapter will clarify the distinction between programming a computer, which requires special skills and knowledge, and using a computer, which needs no more than a short orientation course. It is important to get across to social workers the message that there is no great complexity about using computers, and that the skills they already have need little supplementing. Indeed the additional abilities are equivalent to being able to use a credit card in a slot machine and do simple two-finger typing.

Chapter 6 moves away from the descriptive and specific into the broader context of the social, political and professional issues circumscribing the use of the full technical potential of computers. These issues in turn are enveloped in an ethical debate about the rights and wrongs of employing such powerful systems. One focus is on the memorising capacity of a computer, and the way this can be used to build up massive stores of data about individuals and families. Part of the worry here is simply the scale of operations, the fact that what has replaced traditional filing systems is so much more mind-boggling in its size. Probably more important, however, is the relationship between these big data stores and the state of security in which they are held. Does the system allow too many people access to confidential personal information? Is there illicit access? Are there behind-the-scenes exchanges of information between the organisations controlling data stores? What has happened to traditional professional attitudes towards confidentiality?

A further concern, particularly among those who have used mass data storage, is about its reliability and accuracy. Can computer files be kept sufficiently up to date to be of any use to social workers? And are they? Can they make mistakes in the information that is stored and later revealed? Can we trust this sort of recording as much as older methods? Can it be sufficiently comprehensive, or will it be distorted by the need for brevity and standardisation? There is a phrase in computing, 'garbage in – garbage out', which implies that if computers ever make a mistake it is because fallible humans have offered incorrect material or bad instructions. Is this really so?

Social workers are likely to share the concern about the impact of new technology on employment, both in relation to themselves, and for the possible effect on secretarial and other colleagues. The threat to employment takes specific forms in questions about the precise tasks computers could take over from agency staff. Could computers take on direct interaction with customers, for example, as the duty officer taking initial referral information? Will locally based clerical tasks largely vanish? Are these real threats?

The early developments of computing in the personal social services, with their strong slant towards management uses, had limited appeal to front-line staff because there seemed to be no immediate advantages. Social workers were being asked to fill in rigidly structured forms, designed for a clerk to key in to the computer, but in response to this extra job the computer gave them nothing back, not even a 'thank you'. It remains pertinent for social workers to ask – 'What's in it for us?' – and to go further and wonder about the impact on professional standards and practices, as well as on day-to-day social work activities. Chapter 7 focuses on the social work task, and questions whether a greater use of computers will destroy the 'essence' of social work. Will it damage the personal nature of the work, with its emphasis on the relationships between workers and clients? Does it undermine the principle of treating each client as unique? Will it make social workers more like impersonal service dispensers? The answer to such questions may well depend on the clarity and firmness of social workers' responses to the encroachment of computing, and on their success in gaining a mastery over its application.

The chapter will move on to look at the view that computers just mean extra work for social workers, without, at present, offering much to ease tasks. A central reason for accepting this assessment, at least for a transitory phase lasting several years, is the likelihood that new computerised systems will not be allowed to stand alone until they have proved themselves adequate and reliable for a reasonable trial period. Social workers will therefore be expected, along with their colleagues, to contribute to these new developments while simultaneously maintaining most of the older routines. A big risk is that this transitory phase will become institutionalised into a chronic duplication of functions. An American study (Dery, 1981) has suggested that social workers may be tempted to see a useful opportunity in such duplication. One set of data, a doctored set, is put on the computer for management, so that managers get the picture the field staff want them to have. The other set, kept on traditional locally based files, contains the 'real' records.

There seems to be a widespread acceptance that increasing use will be made of computers in the personal social services, but the likely pace of development is disputed. Advocates of slow development can point to the lack of clarity about the direction of new initiatives, especially in social work practice, and reinforce this view by drawing attention to the scarcity of resources to invest in equipment. The alternative view cites the undoubtedly substantial technical potential for useful computer activity in the agencies. Furthermore, the last decade has been one of innovation in management information systems, and this is now moving into a phase of consolidation. The innovative focus may well switch to social work practice, particularly if the challenge takes the imagination of program (software) writers.

The final chapters look ahead to likely developments in the next few years and decades, so before leaving the present Chapter 7 poses a leading question – Does computerisation work in our personal social services? Is there enough evidence from experience so far to justify moving ahead with confidence, not only into new technology investments, but also into abandoning ways of conducting social work practice and administration which have lasted as long as social work itself?

Chapter 8 looks at the prospect of a decade of development in social work practice, not in general terms so much as in the day-to-day activities of agency staff. Where will computers fit in? What tasks will computers be doing? How will this impinge on social workers' daily work patterns? It is repetitive and tangible tasks that can most easily be set up for computers, so what precisely are the functions under consideration? The creative approach is to see this sort of computer involvement as meeting important needs for the social worker, in strengthening and speeding up the support aspects of the job, so leaving the worker more time for direct work with clients, and providing the information base for a more reflective approach to professional activity. There remains, however, another angle to be recognised. Will the computer be used as an excuse to downgrade social work, and possibly reduce the number of staff? Put another way, will it be used narrowly as a tool for greater productivity, rather than as an opportunity to make a jump forward in the quality of social work performance? Computers could become a boon to the social worker, but there is every risk that in the hands of insensitive political and managerial control they could add to the already high stressfulness of the task.

The last chapter is more speculative, and will crystal-gaze into the more distant prospects for social work. Clearly the computer is not going to be the central catalyst in social work changes. There will be political decisions about the kind of society we are to have, and the meaning that will be given to the term 'Welfare State'. There is no reason to suppose that the relationship of social work to other services will change dramatically, so social work will continue to respond to the dynamics of society, to levels of employment, family breakdown, crime or communal disruption. However, on the assumption that social work will remain a predominantly reactive profession (assuming indeed that it continues as something approaching a 'profession' rather than a social policing employee role), then the computer will need to accommodate to the well-established values of personal service. One specific and relevant change in society can be anticipated – the upsurge in familiarity with computers among the community, and therefore in the customer population. If we can assume familiarity and a willingness to communicate via a computer among people who want personal social service, then the machine will no longer be a block to the establishment of appropriate treatment relationships. The era of keyed-in d-i-y contacts and assessments cannot be far away.

The technology of computing and communicating has progressed with astonishing speed in the last few decades, and there is no reason why it should slow down, so potential is likely to keep its place well ahead of application, and our aspirations will not be held back by technical limitations. One of the achievements of continual miniaturisation in the equipment is to bring down costs. Computing will get progressively cheaper relative to more traditional techniques. It will also become much less realistic to label a computer a 'Dumb 1' (Healey, 1976, p. 41), because the future will bring artificial intelligence. The chapter discusses what we mean by that term and what a computer armed with artificial intelligence capabilities might be in a position to do for social workers and their clients. Perhaps one will become a Director!

1

Computer Myth and Reality

A large part of this chapter will be concerned to start an essential process in any discussion of computing among those who are not specialists in the subject, not part of an 'in-group'. That is de-mystification, clearing away the layers of complexity which impede easy understanding. Complexity surrounds, first of all, the very definition of the term 'computer', which can be used to indicate one specific item of equipment, or as an umbrella label for a range of equipment (hardware) and programs (software). More difficulty stems from the technical language of computing, a jargon which has developed with great rapidity, primarily from American sources, and is a mixture of abbreviations, newly created words and a distorted use of everyday terms.

Once we are clear what we are talking about when referring to a computer and some of the more common terms in the same context, it becomes easier to consider what it is that computers can actually do. This in turn leads up one useful blind alley – indentifying the myths and making clear what cannot be done – but more importantly begs a vital question. What usefulness can computers possibly have for social work?

What is a computer?

There are many introductory books to computing, some offering a decidedly technical approach (for example, Lewin, 1972; Healey, 1976), some aimed at the layman but not shirking some technical aspects (Fry, 1978), and others taking a more discursive line (C.

Evans, 1979). Any reader who wants to investigate the binary system and Boolean algebra (the underpinning of computer architecture), the working of semi-conductors (the basis of computer engineering) or anything else about the intestines of a computer can follow up some of these publications. For all practical purposes there are many things we do not need to know about computers, and which we can add to the general pile of mysteries around us, like what makes refrigerators work or why cocoa will not dissolve in cold water. Simply because computers are part of what we regularly refer to as 'new technology' there is no overriding imperative to strive for total comprehension. Certainly it is fashionable to be able to impress and upstage other people at a meeting, as well as confuse them, by an over-casual recital of technical phrases; but social workers need to see such behaviour for what it is and not be deluded into thinking that there exists some vital area of knowledge and wisdom from which they are excluded. Social workers are not designers or builders of computers, and most likely not writers of programs; they are (potential) computer users, and as such need a relatively uncluttered range of knowledge.

This book will use 'computer' as an umbrella term, covering a whole system, and including the programs or instructions by which the system functions. Technically the computer is the heart of the system (often also called the CPU or central processing unit), while all the other devices around it (the peripheral hardware or peripherals) represent forms of communicating or interacting with the central core. Conceptually that may be a useful way to view the system, but from a practical viewpoint it is deceptive because the peripherals are quite likely not to be visually or physically separate from the CPU. Sometimes they are all in the same cabinet, and with most home computers there is no obvious core or CPU because it is hidden under the keyboard (which conceptually is a peripheral!).

It is helpful to have an image of the CPU as containing three items: a memory store which can be filled with words and figures, a machine for manipulating all the material in the memory and a controller which passes on our instructions about precisely what manipulating shall be undertaken. If we follow certain rules then the controller also has the ability to understand the messages we transmit.

There are numerous devices for communicating with the computer. Some allow us to pass messages (input devices), of which much the best known is the keyboard; this looks, and to a considerable extent behaves, like a conventional typewriter keyboard. Others are for the computer's response (output devices) and include the TV screen (monitor or VDU – visual display unit) and printer. Still more serve both purposes and these are especially concerned with material that is to be stored for later use. There is a limit to the storage capacity of computers, even the very big ones, so when it gets full (or when, with a home or small office computer it is time to switch the power off) extra storage has to be found. This is almost certain to be a cassette recorder, using ordinary cassettes (for the cheaper home computers), or a disk drive, using small flexible plastic disks, like a gramophone record (a 'floppy'), or a bigger thicker disk (a hard disk). These are called input/output (I/O) devices because they can both record transmissions from the computer and play them back again.

A distinction was made earlier between the concept of a computer (defined from now on as the total system) and its visual appearance. It is helpful to hang on to the understanding that conceptually all computers are much the same, though computer specialists might have apoplexy at such an assertion. The purpose of this generalisation is to make the point that the enormous visual disparities do not indicate totally different types of equipment and functioning, and the social worker should take reassurance from knowing that the home computer is really only different in scale (mainly speed of activity and size of memory) from the county council machine. Visually the home computer is small, portable and usually plugs into a TV and cassette recorder which are often used for other purposes. The more expensive personal and small business computers are self-contained desk-top machines, usually with disk storage, because it is quicker, more reliable and has greater capacity, and usually with a screen designed to give a crisper picture and cause less eye strain than conventional TV. Some home computers are made with a restricted use, normally for taking games cartridges only, and some office machines are also limited (or 'dedicated'), most commonly to word-processing. They are still computers, despite the limited range of functions. All of the computers mentioned in the previous sentences could also be accurately called micro-computers, meaning both small-scale and derived from micro-technology (i.e. using micro-processors or chips).

If a computer is not a 'micro' it may be called a mini-computer, though this is becoming an uncommon label and it is more likely to be a 'mainframe'. These very large computers were the first to be designed and produced, and remain those with the largest capacity. Most local authorities and government departments, not to mention other big institutions, will probably have a mainframe computer capable of holding an enormous data store and carrying out a range of tasks. More of this later. Visually a mainframe may well occupy a large space (sometimes air-conditioned to keep the atmosphere dust-free), often out of sight of all but those who work to maintain and operate it. It is the remote terminals, made up of keyboard and screen, which will be the only visible part to most social workers. These terminals may have a direct cable link to the rest of the computer, if it is in the same building; if it is further away, British Telecom provides the connection.

Mention of terminals gives the opportunity to take up a point made in the Introduction – that the technical developments which make possible such labels as 'new technology' are only in part connected with computing. Another important aspect is the growing scope of telecommunications. Together they have been titled 'Information Technology' (IT). Computers store and process the information while communication networks spread it around, so without the transmission potential computers would be restricted to much more localised activity.

As a postcript to this section here is a true story to illustrate the confusion which can be caused by getting immersed in jargon and abbreviation. The author was attending a meeting with officers from a number of agencies to discuss collaboration between social services and education. A social worker took the opportunity to turn the meeting into an impromptu case conference about a 14-year-old boy who was a source of worry. After due deliberation the group decided that what the boy needed was a spell of IT. Over lunch it emerged that the social worker understood this to mean Intermediate Treatment, the education welfare officer anticipated a programme of Industrial Therapy and the boy's head teacher was planning how to find a place on a course in Information Technology.

What can computers do?

The speed and volume of activity will depend on the capacity of the machine. Speed shows itself most clearly in how long the user has to wait for the computer to meet a particular request, though very often if there is a wait the cause of delay lies in one of the peripherals. Cassette recorders and printers are certainly liable to slow down processes and it is generally true that mechanical parts of the computer system work more slowly than electronic parts. There is another way for delays to occur, brought about by the way some computers receive requests from the user. As a community accustomed to home computing we tend to think of computers relating directly and immediately to instructions (being 'interactive'), but many of the older and larger machines were not designed to work in this way. Instead they could only take instructions (via punch cards, for example) in a form which inevitably meant that the user submitted a job, went away and came back later for the results. More to the point, this problem of having to wait for a job to be done, perhaps by joining a queue (often through what is called a 'batch' arrangement) persists with many mainframe computers to the present time. The cause is the need to have a queueing system when there are many users of the same CPU. Jobs can be requested through a keyboard, but if a 'batch' system applies the response may come hours or even days later. Such an arrangement has little if any value for social workers (as the later discussion of Hampshire's developments will indicate), though it may be less inhibiting for managers. For a computer to have any effectiveness in social work practice a pause of maybe thirty seconds in front of a screen will not be troublesome, but a wait of several hours for some case-file information might be impossible to handle. Put the other way round, any computer system which is going to be helpful in social work practice will have to be interactive and immediate ('on-line').

The volume of material a computer can deal with will depend largely on the size of its memory compartment, and how efficiently material can be compressed into it. The big computers have massive memories, way in excess of the needs of any single user, so it is rare for a user even to know what the nominal capacity is. On the other hand micro-computers are almost always described in a way which includes a memory statement. Memory is rated in k-bytes (k standing for kilo) or just plain 'k', and having a big 'k' has become something of a virility symbol among computer buffs. Small micros are probably anything from 16k to 128k, while office machines move rather higher than mere 'k' and into 'm' (for mega-bytes).

In practical terms it is not very helpful to try being precise about how much memory is possible in, say, 1k. The truth will depend on how cleverly designed the specific computer has been to make best use of its memory space, and some will hold a lot more than others. In any event the valid question for social workers is what sort of speed and capacity would be needed to handle a single caseload, an area team's workload or the whole agency load? It has already been argued that the vital factor about speed is being 'on-line', and that memory size is not going to be an issue with a mainframe computer. This leaves only the memory capacity of micro-computers to consider, and this has to be related to other factors, such as how quickly a particular machine can call in some material from a connected 'off-line' store (a disk drive), and whether the material in the computer's memory is all going to be needed simultaneously, or bit-by-bit, in sequence. There is no helpful generalised answer.

Moving on from the specific questions of how much and how fast, and back to the theme of 'What can computers do?', the next part of the answer is that they can only, in theory, do what they are asked to do – providing they have the ability to do it. At this point 'ability' should be understood as covering rather different areas to those considered earlier under the theme of 'capacity'. That is to say, it is not concerned with the internal electronic potential and limits of the equipment, which has already been touched on when discussing such topics as memory size. Ability here refers primarily to the degree of success with which user and computer can communicate. The variations are great. Some computers can only respond if the user issues instructions of a specific kind in a rigidly predetermined format. Other machines are more tolerant in the range of communication they can understand, or are designed to help the user get the format correct by reporting what is wrong and indicating how it can be altered. The concept here is described as 'user-friendliness', and it is usually the smaller systems which have been designed to be most 'user-friendly'. Indeed there is something of a gulf in design between the larger computers, where it is assumed that they will be operated by experts, and the bulk of micro-computers, which have to cope with experts and amateurs, as well as those of us who want to be users but have no urge to comprehend the intricate intestines.

The assertion that computers can only do what they are instructed to do is a long-established dogma. At a time when there was no working computer, and nothing more than a plan for an 'Analytical Engine', Lord Byron's daughter, Lady Ada Lovelace, was writing firmly that it 'has no pretensions whatever to originate anything. It can do whatever we know how to order it to perform. It can follow analysis; but it has no power of anticipating any analytical relations or truths'. (Lovelace, 1842, note G.) The same basic message has been repeated ever since, and it has a characteristic which has already been noted about some computing principles. It is useful as a concept, but riddled with holes if we want to use it as a working guideline. Leaving aside for the moment any query about the soundness of the principle, its apparent simplicity and neutrality covers up important issues. The computer may only be able to do what it is told, but it can receive instructions in different ways, from different people, at different times. At the design and production stage it can be given instructions which are built into the machine and cannot be countermanded by later orders. The same potential exists when programs are lodged in the machine for (semi-) permanent use. As will be seen later in Chapter 3, this facility is regularly used, for example in setting up security systems for local authority computers.

The important point for social workers, and indeed anyone else who may want computers to do tasks with confidential information, is to avoid falling into the trap of seeing the principle of giving/receiving orders as implying a unique and discrete relationship between themselves and the computer they are using. There are other users or others who can get into the position, legitimately or not, of giving instructions, so although the computer will only do what it is told it may not have been YOU who did the telling. Furthermore computers, especially the smaller ones, can have accidents. There are all sorts of unavoidable causes – dust, static electricity, a flash of lightning or coffee leaking down through the keyboard. Often these will provoke nothing more than a passing hiccup; but they can lead the machine to freeze up or start emitting a mass of incoherent rubbish, and just occasionally the accident gets interpreted by the computer as a recognisable instruction, which it then carries out. None of this is intended to stir up alarm, because it can easily be incorporated into the user's expectations of the equipment and programmes. Rather it is aimed to dispel the idea that because a computer 'only does what it is told' it has some kind of infallibility. Any social worker who has used a computer, large or small, will know only too well how fallible they are. There are, of course, ethical, political and practical dimensions to this fallibility (and to intentional abuse) all of which will be discussed in later chapters.

There is a more restricted way of expressing the relationship between computer and user which has totally dependable outcomes. It is contained in the phrase 'garbage in – garbage out' (GIGO), a wholly reliable rule that if the user puts inaccurate material into the computer then the computer will give inaccurate material back.

A computer has no difficulty in handling any material composed of words and/or figures (alphanumeric data), so given the necessary instructions there is nothing in conventional social work records which could not be stored. Charts and diagrams can also be keyed in. The tasks the computer can accomplish with this material can be categorised into a number of general functions:

1. Provide safe storage.
2. Repeat back the data on demand.
3. Enable the data to be changed (edited).
4. Search the data to find a particular item.
5. Search for 'look alike' material.
6. Rearrange the format/presentation of the data.
7. Undertake 'secondary analysis', to offer composite data.

There are other more specialised functions, but those listed are likely to be found in any system. These, and more tailor-made applications, will be followed through at later stages in the book. However, it should be noted that no suggestion has been made about computers thinking for themselves, which after all is precluded within the rule of 'following orders'. Computers do not have independent minds, but the idea of the 'thinking computer' is no longer pure fantasy, and there are developments of artificial intelligence. These have not spread to social work, and are not likely to in the foreseeable future, but they will be touched on in a speculative final chapter. Social workers are not in the vanguard of computer applications, and there is a decade or more of technical development to employ in the personal social services before the latest innovations are reached.

Why should social workers use computers?

First a word of clarification is called for about 'use' in this context. Most uses to date have been connected with the administration of services, primarily with overall agency management, but with extensions into more localised caseload management. There are specific arguments for and against this form of usage. However there has already been discussion in these pages, and there will be much more, about computer use in social work practice. In so far as this brings computers directly into the working relationship between social worker and client, a new set of arguments are appropriate. Issues specific to computers in social work practice will be left to later chapters, and this section will focus on general arguments and those concerned with administrative activities. There is a rational to this approach. It is a clear observation that computers have gained their foothold in social services departments in order to help with administrative tasks, while practice developments have followed on or been held in abeyance. This reflects (or can be rationalised to reflect!) a gradual organic introduction of computing into agency processes. It also indicates a higher level of experience and greater sense of security about some uses as contrasted with others. It would seem sensible, therefore, at least as a first stage, for arguments to be based on the central body of experience, rather than on more speculative experimental or possible future uses.

The roots of the argument have two strands: one linked to dissatisfaction with traditional methods, the other to kowledge about the technical possibilities of computing. The critique of older forms of administration have less to do with any intrinsic weaknesses than with their inability to cope with changing circumstances. Those changes included dramatic increases in agency size, so that the total volume of agency data, especially client files and information about resources, was suddenly too large to be handled by manual systems. Close on the heels of the formation of bigger agencies came a winding down of an era of comfortable growth, and the imposition of ever-tighter systems of budgeting and resource deployment. Once again manual methods were found not to be taut enough, or sometimes sufficiently fast-acting to meet new pressures.

There remains a sound alternative to bringing in computers, and that is to avoid increases in agency size, and keep to proportions which can be handled in traditional ways. Over the last couple of decades it has gained little headway because the values of big-scale and high-powered management have held sway. Computers have not been neutral in all this. Their existence has made it possible to think big, and give plausibility to the whole philosopohy. However, if we are prepared to accept as a permanent feature that our agencies are now relatively large organisations and big spenders, it becomes logical to accept computing as a necessary tool. If personal social services agencies had not thought about, and in most instances taken on, some computing facility, there would have been a degree of isolation from other local authority and central government services. Indeed it is agencies which have been characterised by small size and a clear sense of separate identity (often probation and aftercare services) in which traditional practices have been best able to endure.

These are desultory and somewhat lack-lustre arguments for using computers, in a context of inevitability rather than enthusiasm. There are fervent supporters and equally strong opponents. On the one hand computers have been called the 'next great turning-point which mankind is rapidly approaching' (C. Evans, 1979, p. 12); while in contrast they have been seen as a 'monstrous system of "total administration" that cancels out man, not through terror and brutal authoritarianism, but through gradual subjugation' (Gruber, 1974, p. 625). In the social work services published comments have been more reticent:

> In principle, new technology in social services departments offers a valuable opportunity to relieve social workers of much of the clerical and administrative drudgery which deflects them from direct contact with clients and the exercise of their distinctive professional skills. . . . In practice, experience is varied! (NALGO, 1984, p. 44).

Within the social services there have, for many years, been small groups of enthusiasts, participating in organisations like LAMSAC and BURISA (British Urban and Regional Information System Association). Yet the predominant impression from talking to social workers has been one of suspicion and scepticism, and the arguments for using computers have been stated in that sort of tone to reflect such attitudes. Despite signs of change there remains a widespread feeling among social workers that computing does not have much to offer them, and certainly nothing like as much as it offers managers. Such views will need to change before it becomes possible to put the case for computers with both conviction and gusto.

2

The Growth of Computing in Social Work Services

Computers have developed from calculating-machines, and because, through most of our history, ideas and plans have outstripped the capability of production engineering, it is easier to look back and find designs for computers than working models. It is usual to identify two of the great philosophers, Pascal and Leibniz, both from the seventeenth century, as the first conceivers of calculating-machines. Charles Babbage, in the nineteenth century, came nearer to a design for a computer. His Analytical Engine has a format similar to a modern computer, with a CPU (he called it a 'Mill') incorporating a memory. He also conceived the idea of putting information into the Engine via punched cards, and linking a printer to receive the output. However, there were no electronics in his day, so the design was entirely mechanical. He received a little government development money, but precision engineering techniques were not up to the job, and the Engine could not be built. 'He was born one hundred years too soon.' (Healey, 1976, p. 29.)

For the next few decades computing returned to the realms of ideas and designs, but it was an important phase because it carried through the conceptual transformation of calculator into computer. Babbage (who was a Professor of Mathematics at Cambridge University) had suggested a move away from making specific requests for specific calculations towards the idea of a programme of instructions, incorporating both a sequence of activities and the possibility of flexibility along the lines of – 'if this occurs then go along that path, but if it doesn't then take a different course'. Extensions of these ideas led to the image we have today of a computer as a flexible programmable machine, capable of handling almost any type of material, and certainly not confined to numbers. At the same time there was evident frustration that ways of putting theories into practice, first mechanically, then electrically, and finally electronically were so inadequate until the 1940s. Mass production in these early years focused much more on mechanical calculators, especially after the boost given to them by the US Census Bureau. In the 1880s the Bureau, worried that the next ten-yearly Census would take place before the results of the previous one were available, had a competition to find the best way of calculating the 1890 results. Hermann Hollerith won easily, got the job, got a lot more jobs as interest grew in the business community, and helped to set up the International Business Machine Corporation – IBM, the giant of the computer industry. His successor at IBM put up a million dollars to build the first genuine computer – the Harvard Mark 1.

These early machines were colossal, expensive, had long spells out of action and were wholly incomprehensible to all but a few specialists. The revolution between the 1940s and the present has been caused not so much by new ideas on computing as new inventions in electronics – the transistor and the micro-processor especially – which have brought the small, competent low-priced equipment we know today.

What, the reader might pertinently ask, has all of this got to do with social work? The answer is to draw the obvious conclusions about the incredible rate of technical development, and equally astonishing reductions in size, complexity and cost of computing, and to point out that these must have implications for all organisations, with no exemptions for social workers. The answer is also to focus attention on the continuing pioneering activity that characterises such rapid growth, and note the qualities of imagination, inventiveness and experimentation which are present in abundance. How forcefully this contrasts with the apathy and suspicion of many social workers, as mentioned in the last chapter.

Computers in the personal social services

Managers in the services have been less apathetic, and have been using computers for over a decade. There was some small use before 1971, but the real impetus came from the formation of social services departments, coupled with the simultaneous rise in statutory work and the increased range and volume of circumstances recognised as 'needs'. Indeed a persistent difficulty for social services departments has been the contrast between the seemingly endless scope for needs to expand and the limits placed on the growth of resources. The rise in demand through the 1970s, sometimes running at an annual rate of 25–30 per cent (documented in Sainsbury, 1977), cannot be explained solely by analysing the nature of human needs, since, in crucial ways, social services departments have developed a new perspective on service provision. It is, perhaps, a justifiable generalisation to suggest that traditional social work has been preoccupied with the quality of interaction between worker and client, and less concerned with issues of quantity. Social services departments set out to redress this imbalance, to facilitate a high standard of work and at the same time meet, in so far as resources permitted, the span and scale of expressed needs. The themes which have emerged, in consequence, are broadly similar to those which have been found in other welfare sectors, such as the Health Service. How can the volume of service output be maximised, while maintaining acceptable standards of performance? Can short-term methods of treatment be developed so that the turnover of clients is speeded up? Are there ways of improving staff productivity? Can we operate humane and sensible forms of rationing to deal with the apparently inevitable disparity between demand and supply?

The importance of finding answers to these questions is sufficient justification for examining ways of improving the effectiveness of social work administration. To many managers it seemed obvious that computers might be a helpful tool, particularly when faced with breakdowns in traditional procedures under the weight of expansion. A London-based study concluded that social workers 'consider their efforts to be almost as frequently hindered as helped by existing administrative procedures' (Pascoe, 1978). It cited a number of complaints about the reaction of manual systems to pressure:

Too much paperwork
Difficulties in information retrieval
Poor arrangements for circulating information

Information not kept up to date
No standardised and widely understood system.

In the US similar experiences have pushed agencies towards computing. Schoech and Arangio (1979) suggest four categories of motivation: standardisation, getting bigger information systems, having the ability to evaluate projects and aiding better service co-ordination. Another comment on the US scene asserts that 'many manual information systems are no longer adequate to meet the increasingly complex data demands which are being placed on agencies. Often the data needed to make decisions is not collected, or if collected, it is stored in such a way that useful retrieval is extremely difficult.' (Schoech, Schkade and Mayers, 1982, p. 12.)

The earliest computer installations in British social work services just preceded the formation of social services departments, but the flurry in the 1970s was very much a response to the new departments, or to the increases in size following local government reorganisation in 1974. One of the first reports on the experience (Derbyshire, 1974) discussed five computer systems, without claiming that these were the only ones. The earliest had its origins in Lancashire's Children's Department. The most recent survey (LAMSAC, 1982) found that all local authorities responding to a questionnaire (96 out of 125) had some central computing facility, and over three-quarters (74 of the 96) had specific applications for their social services departments. Several of the remainder had plans in hand.

The rapid expansion in the number of computer systems in operation has not been matched by comparable changes in the objectives and functions of the programs. Derbyshire's study suggested four frequent uses:

1. Management information
2. DHSS Annual Returns
3. Operational or *ad hoc* information
4. Rationalising records

By the 1980s there had been some change of emphasis, noticeably in the way annual returns had become an integrated taken-for-granted aspect of the wider processing network, and much more sophistication could be found. Yet the only substantially new preoccupation, and a clear reflection of the changing economic circumstances over the decade, was with using computers for budgetary control and monitoring. Except for a growing scope for social workers in the front line to have access to the data store of client records and resources, there was little sign of computer functions spreading much beyond the management scene. In particular only five authorities had developed micro-computer applications for anything other than word-processing in their social services departments (LAMSAC, 1982, para. 3).

What sort of computer systems?

The large majority of social services departments use mainframe computers, shared with other local authority departments. Very often the sharing arrangement is with longer-standing users, so that the systems themselves may have been installed with these other users in mind. Most commonly they are the departments handling central accountancy, personnel and payroll functions (LAMSAC, 1982). This has had a number of implications for social service uses. When a computer already exists in the local authority, and it has spare capacity, the social services committee is hardly likely to give a high priority to buying new equipment for a different type of system. There were obvious economies, or so there seemed, in having a slot in the existing machine. The real price to be paid was that the system was not necessarily appropriate for social services, especially where it involved small departments buying space on large (and possibly dated) computers. The sort of space on offer might itself not be suitable if it could not be utilised to give an immediate (on-line) response to requests, and this was one of the most important weaknesses of early developments. Put in a slightly more political way, social services, as newcomers, could not expect any privileges, and would always come further back in the queue than established users. This has been most noticeable when major policy decisions have had to be taken about, for example, equipment replacement. Finally the sharing itself carried the seed of dissent and controversy, because it so blatantly set up the possibility of data sharing, of allowing other departments and agencies to get hold of confidential case files.

The development of purpose-designed computer systems for the personal social services has shown some distinct differences to the schemes which were cobbled on to existing computers. The best-known of the early systems is SOSCIS (SOcial Services Client Information System), which was developed in Gateshead between 1974 and 1977, using a large ICL computer. Gateshead's circumstances were in many ways typical of those discussed earlier. Local government reorganisation had more than doubled the catchment population of the social services department. Traditional administrative methods were collapsing under the pressure – there was not enough standardisation and no quick or easy access to information, case files were inconveniently located and liable to get lost and management felt disadvantaged by the absence of cumulative and comparative data (Eason, 1982). The local authority (not the social services department) had decided on the purchase of a big new computer. It is pertinent to ask just how different SOSCIS would have been if its developers had not been forced to react to urgent pressures or to share a computer.

The answer to that question may well come from looking at one of the small number of systems which have been purpose-designed for personal social service tasks, without having to consider the needs of other departments. An example is PROBIS, the PROBation Information System developed and made available through the Home Office Research and Planning Unit. An initial point to note is that probation departments are generally smaller than social services, and it is no accident that the temptation to purpose-develop comes from that end of the size spectrum. Systems like SOSCIS will certainly be less attractive to the smaller agencies, mainly because they are likely to be expensive to set up and operate on a small scale.

PROBIS is micro-computer based, and hence makes use of more modern technology. It also presupposes that it will be the only programme operating on the equipment, since the capacity of the machines to be installed is calculated from the anticipated size of the PROBIS information store. Hence it removes fears of contamination or muddling with other data files and other users –

fears which exist even if computer specialists assert that they are groundless.

The opportunities offered by PROBIS, SOSCIS and most of the other systems in use around the country have broad similarities. They all store information relevant to the agency, about clients, services offered, resources available and in use, budgets, staff, staff workloads, known risks and so forth. The difference between systems is that whereas the more limited schemes are selective about the information stored, focusing on what management considers to be high priority, the more comprehensive ones (usually newer) aim to establish an 'all-in' file, often with internal categories, but in an overall context of the computer becoming the repository of the agency's information. A big task (and headache!) for all the systems, but especially the more substantial ones, is keeping the information up to date. The problem of out-of-date information has already been mentioned as a characteristic of manual systems, as well as potentially of computer-based ones, and any system requires an effective, accurate and quick way for adding to or altering files. A difficulty at the other end of the process which is exacerbated by computation, can be caused by the system getting cluttered up with data no longer needed, especially if it fills limited memory space.

All the computer systems are designed to make the stored data available to management, whether in raw form or after analysis. Dery (1981) makes a point about this: 'the central information issue is not how many data there are, or how fast they can be retrieved, but, rather, whether . . . we not only create data-rich worlds but also help management to get what it wants or needs, and thereby convert data into information' (p. 9). This is a controversial statement, heavily biased towards a management viewpoint. Keeping the distinction he makes between data and information, data may be of little use to managers until it is processed into information, but data (by which we mean mostly material about individual clients or circumstances) is the life-blood of the front-line practitioner. It is a foretaste of debate to come later that managers are more bothered about the quality of material after it has been analysed, while social workers will have greater need of the raw data. These needs are not always in harmony.

In its most limited format the information offered by the computer system (please forget now any subtle distinctions between information and data!) will be for managers only, and possibly supplied only with a slow turn-around (as on a batch system). The development offered by SOSCIS and most of the more recent programmes makes the information available quickly (on-line), and it can be directed to several outlets, so that it becomes a resource for social work practitioners. The next chapter will contain a much more detailed look at topics which have been summarised in previous paragraphs, since Hampshire's computer history moves from initial limited managerial aims through to a sophisticated agency wide computer network.

A rational approach to computer use

This brief look at some of the factors in the history of computer uses in social services departments tends towards the conclusion that pressure and opportunity played a large part, with careful design and reflection often some way behind. A more careful approach is often advocated, sometimes a more cautious one (as by LAMSAC's Social Services Computer Applications Group, reported in *Community Care*, 17 February 1983). Emphasis is likely to be placed too on responsibility – 'it is the responsibility of administrators not only to recognise and exploit the capabilities of the modern computer ... but to comprehend the impact of the computer on staff at all levels ... the administrator must view the computer broadly' (Hoshino, 1982, p. 5). Arguments of a general kind for using computers have already been aired, but is there a more specific process which can amount to a rational, thorough and realistic feasibility check? The relevance of such a check has been observed. 'The notion of feasibility is one that is critical to the implementation of a formal information system, particularly one that will or does include a computer.' (LaMendola, 1982, p. 43.)

A number of planning stages can be identified. Given that a computer installation is an expensive item, the first steps should involve the pre-computer schemes:

1. A check to discover the level of effectiveness of the existing

information system, leading to an itemised list of weaknesses and another list of valued characteristics which must be obtainable in any replacement system.

2. A statement of the contents of the data-files, the categories of files and the volume of material.

3. An estimate of expected changes to the agency's information, whether originating from changes in agency policies or external circumstances. It is helpful for this to include some comment on desired surplus capacity.

4. A statement of information turnover, including expected daily/weekly amounts to be added and the speed with which entries are required, as well as the volume and rate of data discards. Is data simply deleted or a transfer arrangement wanted to an inactive file?

5. A statement of information use. What is the level and nature of transactions? Facts are needed about the daily/weekly number of requests for information from the files, and the type of requests which are made (for case-file access, composite tables, secondary analysis and so forth). An estimate is needed of likely changes in use, especially if improved access arrangements are being considered, or the addition of more potential users.

6. A calculation of time needed for different uses, which at least specifies the ratios between data input, deletion, search and analysis. Precise timings may not be helpful if consideration is being given to major changes in operation, for example from a card index system to a computer, but ratios and an attempt at an overall estimate are needed to aid calculating the scale of any new equipment (number of computer keyboards, for example).

7. A ranked list of the essential characteristics and the functions of any new system, drawing not only on the virtues of what is being replaced, but also on what agency staff have identified as necessary for future developments.

While it may be helpful to have an idea of what a computer can do if the ranked list is to be realistic, it is only once this preliminary information is established that the possibility of computers comes into the reckoning, initially in comparison with alternative prospects.

8. Examine the potential for altering or extending the existing

information system to overcome known weaknesses and meet anticipated needs. If the potential exists, cost it.

9. Report on the technical feasibility of different systems, to clarify which can offer, with ease and convenience, the characteristics and functions needed. Include capacity and scope for expansion. Flexibility is also worth consideration. The suggestion here is to do this exercise for different systems, meaning more than one computerised arrangement. At a minimum this should include one mainframe- or mini-computer-based scheme, and one using micro-computers.

10. Report on the 'image' of any proposed system. What does it look like? What space will it take up? How accessible will it be? Will it be attractive for current and possible future users, in the sense of being 'user-friendly'?

11. Produce costings, to include equipment, installation, maintenance and replacement. Budgets are also needed for space, staffing, staff training and routine running.

At this point the concerns move into areas of economic feasibility and away from the intended subject-matter of this book. However, a process such as has been itemised here can serve useful purposes. Most obviously it puts calculations and estimates about computer applications within the same planning context as other possibilities for information handling, which is a more rational approach than assuming that computers must be better because they are new and fashionable. In addition a logical approach has much more prospect of convincing the doubters, especially among social workers, that decisions have been soundly based, at least at a technical, economic and administrative level. It means that these practical factors do not muddy the water when we try to clarify the political, professional and ethical aspects of computer use.

Installing computer systems

There is, in outline, a clear sequence to installation. It begins with moving in the equipment (hardware), linking it together, which is not always easy, and checking that it works. Next the overall system instructions (the programs – software) can be incorporated, and trial runs can begin. Writing a program for a computer has a three-step sequence – designing the program, writing it and then getting it to run smoothly and effectively (debugging). Most debugging is done once the program is running in the computer, because it is only by trial runs that many of the flaws can be discovered and wrinkles ironed out. Even if the program works well there may still be more work to do, because there is a quality to programming which is akin to literary style. A message can be conveyed in a clumsy, long-winded and unattractive way, and still be understood; but it can also be expressed with panache, brevity and beauty. The most flattering comment a computer specialist can pass on a program is to call it 'elegant'!

The final stage of the installation process is to move into full operation, which does not in theory seem a very difficult task, though many agencies have agonised over it, and few have tackled it comprehensively. The problem lies less in the computer itself than in our frequent but not always justified mistrust of it. During the trial stages it is sensible to retain the previous information system as a backup. The big hurdle to overcome is to discard the backup once the computer is fully operational. In practice many social services departments have opted to keep a permanent backup, to institutionalise their doubts about the dependability of computers. It is a costly decision, and a sort of information obsession.

During the process of installation, whether of 'off-the-shelf' or newly devised computer systems, there are a couple of factors which particularly affect social workers. The previous paragraph got close to one of them, in mentioning the mistrust of computers. It is the tendency of the system to sporadic inaccuracies and oddities which are especially likely to occur during the early months, and may never vanish altogether. The inaccuracies are likely to be in specific bits of data, and although there will be exceptions, they can usually be explained by reference to the 'garbage in – garbage out' principle. The oddities may be more dramatic, and are more likely to be the result of 'bugs' in the system. A screen display of total rubbish is one sign, as is the seeming inability of the computer to carry on doing what you have instructed. Just occasionally (very rarely indeed, if the truth is told) a user asks for some simple bit of information and instead breaks into a juicy confidential file!

Bugs need to be cleared out, but some of the problem over

inaccuracies stems from social workers' attitudes. Under the old manual regimes social workers took it for granted and in their stride that files or file entries would go missing, or be unreadable and untrue. Why is it that the moment a computer comes into operation our expectations change, and we look for perfection? Computers are far from perfect, but they are a lot more accurate at storing and retrieving information than their manual predecessors.

The remaining installation difficulty for social workers is the communication gulf between those who know how to do social work and those who know about computers. There are very few people who combine that knowledge. This is especially a problem when the computer is a large one or is situated in another department, because in those circumstances the computer will be run by specialist staff whose training and experience may have involved no contact whatsoever with the personal social services. On the other side, the use of computers is not yet considered an essential part of the curriculum for social work training, and in-service induction courses will, quite reasonably, focus on the functional specifics of 'being a user'. The interdisciplinary communication task presents a big challenge for the future, and the next chapter will relate how one large social services department is trying to meet it.

3

Computing in One Social Services Department

Hampshire Social Services Department (from now on 'the Social Services') covers the entire county of Hampshire. It is a large department, with a population catchment of over one and a half million people. In 1971, when the Social Services Act came into operation, there were three independent social services departments, in the county of Hampshire and the county boroughs of Portsmouth and Southampton. The boroughs were the main urban centres, but were nevertheless a lot smaller than the county. A proposal that as part of the local authority reorganisation planned for 1974 the three councils should merge into one was strenuously opposed at a political level, partly because the boroughs were fearful of being swamped, partly on account of the party political make-up. The county has a tradition of Conservative management, whereas the boroughs have shown more tendency to waver. A combined authority would have a built-in Conservative majority.

The merger duly occurred in 1974 and since then there has been regular discussion about reversing the process and re-establishing the old boroughs. There is no evidence in the Social Services that this debate has affected planning, and the process of integration into a single agency, slow at first, has gained pace in the early 1980s. Whether the level of services has fallen below that which the boroughs might have wanted is more debatable. The county gets a tick, a star and a pat on the back from the Conservative government at Westminster for its adherence to expenditure limits, though it may well not receive such favourable backing from the (now) district councils of the two south-coast cities.

Any political worries which might have existed in the three

social services departments were kept well beneath the surface, though concern about the new structure and the rearrangement of jobs was widely discussed. In the event the new Social Services represented the minimum disruption, possibly at the price of a managerial framework which was cumbersome, costly and hierarchical. The old boroughs, with additions to their geographic peripheries, because Divisions, as did the remainder of the county. Superimposed on the divisions was a new HQ in the county town, Winchester. This framework was given nearly a decade to settle, and consolidate its work patterns before a further round of administrative restructuring began with the removal of the divisional headquarters. Only recently, therefore, has Hampshire switched from an atypical three-tier structure (HQ – Divisions – Areas) to the more usual two-tier arrangement (HQ – Areas).

The purpose of this historical summary is to identify a number of factors which influenced the growth of a computer system. One point has already been noted – that the Social Services has a large catchment population. It also covers a large geographical area, with as much as fifty road miles separating the distant points. The fact that it is made up of three different social services departments, which only a few years before were themselves amalgamations, resulted in a wide range of different practices and information systems. Political sensitivity has perhaps led to careful attention to the provision of data upon which the Department's performance can be judged, with some emphasis on being able to provide an effective factual backup service to any issue under political debate. Lastly, the long-drawn-out process of administrative reorganisation has forced some tailoring of the computer system.

Origins of the computer system

The initial thrust to the Hampshire computer development came from the decision to merge Portsmouth and Southampton with the county of Hampshire on 1 April 1974, and to negotiate a gradual integration towards a new Social Services Department. It undoubtedly helped in this fraught exercise that the Director and several of the new HQ staff came from one or other of the boroughs, with an understanding of their circumstances and feelings, because it did appear that it was the boroughs which were being expected to make the biggest changes and to lose their status. An essential early phase of the plan to get the Social Services working as a coherent unit was a look at existing administrative systems. A Records Procedures Working Party found a chaotic situation. In outline the working party found three broadly different record systems, each with eccentricities derived largely from *ad hoc* responses to national (DHSS) and local demands as they arose. Within the three systems were sixty-four different locations of records, again frequently having their own localised characteristics. The methods of storage varied, both in substantial ways (like the content of files) and in ways which were minor but irritating (like the size of index cards). The purposes for which files were held varied, from card indexes kept up at considerable cost for use only in preparing annual returns, to full operational case files. The subject-matter about which data were held also lacked any consistent pattern, and there was extensive duplication. It was not uncommon for a client to have more than one file, assembled quite independently, in different places. About the only thing the systems had in common was that they were all manual, and tended to be slow and cumbersome to use.

At this time the county had an under-used computer (main-frame), with a computer staff who were interested in the prospects of extending their range of activities. The outcome was inevitable. The working party recommended that a single-records system should be established in each division, standardised both within and between divisions – effectively a single system, with data accumulated at three points in the department. Further it was recommended that the county computer should be used, and a small group of staff from the computer section and Social Services got together to make, and later implement, specific proposals. The objectives of a computer-based system were twofold:

a) the standardisation of the existing record systems, thus providing the Department with an information base common to all three Divisions;

b) the storage and retrieval of information sufficient for Annual Returns and any other management information, thus eliminating the need for duplicate or parallel sets of index cards used solely in compiling DHSS returns. (First Report on the Introduction of a Divisional Computer-Based Information System, April 1974.)

It is perhaps helpful at this stage to pause and clarify just what was and was not involved in this proposal, since it would be a mistake to blanket in all agency records. The focus was clearly and explicitly on such records as would be needed by management for specific managerial purposes and annual returns, primarily for DHSS, but also for the Social Services Committee. Although client case-files and case-recording in parts of Hampshire were about to become the subject of study by the National Institute for Social Work (more later on this), files compiled by social workers for social work purposes were not included. Indeed the role of social workers would be to provide data for the computer store, without any opportunity either to understand the system or make direct use of it, though some data analysis would be available for them. The aim of management at this stage was to disturb social workers as little as possible. Hampshire's computer system needs to be seen as one which grew in a series of steps, and the big step of involving social workers and social work practice came a few years later.

The First Report mentioned above discussed the pros and cons of the proposals. The undeniable advantages were that the system would overcome confusion in the records, save time in the current level of information analysis, especially annual returns, make more information available in forms useful to managers and cope with the volume of data held by a big department. A more general argument was made about the greater flexibility of a computer file over a card index, both in editing (changing or keeping up to date) and secondary analysis. This latter point was reinforced by the expectation that output from the computer would include (for the first time) an analysis of data categorised by area and available to area offices, as well as an '*ad hoc* query' service.

Costing for the system came out favourably. There would be a need for some extra clerical staff to handle the backlog and get the data file set up, but in the long run the Group expected a saving over the cost of the existing arrangements. This calculation was aided by quite favourable terms for the purchase of time on the county computer, and the early plan involved very little capital investment in equipment by the Social Services. That came later.

The budgetary arguments were perhaps slightly distorted because the computer estimates were compared to existing manual system costs, not to estimates for a streamlined manual scheme (for example, a microfiche file).

A rather more general economic argument was suggested in a separate planning document, which as well as giving specific cost details added: 'In the present climate of economic stringency, the review of service delivery ... and the assessment of the effectiveness of services provided must clearly be of considerable importance, and the proposed system is intended to provide the data base for such activity.' (Computer Development Group internal document of 1974.) This comment is set more in the context of an advertising puff for computerisation than as part of a discussion of a sensitive issue. Yet it was, and soon became accepted as one of the more fraught aspects of developing ever wider information and analysis capabilities. The prospect of the computer being used as a means of overseeing and monitoring fieldwork, or as a tool of fiscal retrenchment, was certain to make it unpopular in parts of the agency. Furthermore it fuelled the tendency to resent the computer as an instrument of control and power. To an outside observer throughout this phase of the Social Services' computer history it was noticeable that this sort of resentment grew and continued among social workers, until in a later development it was decided to inform, involve and consult field staff.

The only disadvantage acknowledged in the planning documents was the (as it turned out transitory) snag of delays in the output from the computer. However, others were around and recognised. One, which subsequently grew to parallel, perhaps to exceed, the 'control' fears, was the worry about confidentiality and the security of computer files. Security techniques will be discussed later in this chapter, but it is arguable that the computer has been unfairly blamed for a widespread lapse in traditional attitudes towards confidentiality. The very formation of social services departments increased the number of staff with authorised access to files, regardless of the use of computers. Another concern, which has been more narrowly contained within the staff group operating the Social Services computer activity, was with the relationship with the more powerful computer users in the local authority. In the early days there was perhaps some of the insecurity which commonly surrounds a new development, but there is a more lasting element which can have the effect of reducing Social Services' flexibility. As long as they remained small users there were few difficulties, but the Social Services staff found that with the expansion of the system tension points increased with other users.

The Group recommended implementation of their proposals over a surprisingly short period. The proposals themselves were put forward in April, with the recommendation that the system could be operational by mid-October. Confidence was not misplaced, and the system was giving output before the end of 1974.

The management information system

When the Social Services system first became operational it was geared to accommodate data on 33 000 current case records and 20 000 home-help records. Projecting from the manual scheme, it was expected that there would be about 15 000 entries to the computer per year (a few new files, but mainly changes and additions to existing files). Output was anticipated at about fifty tables for annual DHSS returns, some committee statistics and perhaps five inquiries each week. It needs to be emphasised that these figures assumed a level of activity comparable with the past, whereas in reality the introduction of the computer began a rapid and continuing phase of growth in the size, range and use of the information system.

Building up the data files took longer than was expected, but the backlog had been dealt with by the end of 1975, and a description of the system in mid-1976 (Wilshire, 1976) saw it broadly as containing three elements. Two parts combined to form the Management Information System itself. These were the client files and the establishment files. The client files did not include all the cases of social workers and other front-line staff, but only those with 'management implications'. This was in keeping with past tradition, and incorporated those cases where there was either a specific legal requirement or an allocation of agency resources (other than a bit of social worker time). The establishment files set out to list Social Services resources, in residential and day-care services, foster homes, play groups, child minders and a number of other sectors. It also included private and voluntary establishments registered with the department.

The third component, described as the Referral Recording System, was intended partly to plug the gap in the client files and ensure that note was made of all referrals to area centres. Much the largest group were the elderly. There was, however, a more substantial element to this development. Since 1973 the National Institute for Social Work, with a team of workers led by Tilda Goldberg, had been analysing data collection documents and feeding in recommendations to the Social Services. Out of this research came the Case Review System (see Goldberg and Warburton, 1979), which was later taken on by Hampshire's computer division, and subsequently by other local authorities. In the event it did not retain a separate identity in Hampshire, or receive much development, but was merged into the expanding client files. Already it was acknowledged that: 'The true core of this information base is the Management Information System. It is this system that will provide the majority of information for the department in future.' (Wilshire, 1976.) The Case Review System had not been developed through a study of needs at HQ, but by linking with social workers and other front-line staff in an area team. As such it was probably too sensitive to the concerns of social workers to gain the necessary priority at that stage of computer applications.

Entries both to client and establishment files were initiated by an action note from area office or other front-line venue, passed to division, which in turn transferred the information to an input form. There was a form each for client or establishment entry, but the same form covered new referrals, changes to existing files and closures. The forms were then gathered at the divisional offices and sent in bundles to HQ for putting on to the computer. A temporary computer file was created and a copy of the proposed entry returned for correction to the division, and only after that was it put (at fortnightly intervals) on to the permanent file. Both forms included basic factual data which would be useful for annual returns, statistical analysis and outline data searches, but excluded any comment or qualitative material, or any record of social worker involvement (through the reference number of the client's social worker was included, along with 'aids provided'). Similarly the establishment files did not include anything which might portray the 'flavour' of the entry. Some parts of the forms (like addresses) could simply be written in, while others (like the area office and social worker) had to be entered as a code number. This meant that anyone using the computer needed a code book for translation purposes.

Computer jobs were dealt with by a batch method, which is to say that there was no immediate interaction with the computer, and 'processing' time could be as much as two days for some work. This was not a problem for annual returns and statistical analysis, but made urgent searches impossible. Hence the computer had great flexibility if there was enough time – it could produce almost any kind of analysis as well as other helpful bits and pieces, like sticky address labels for all addresses lodged on the establishment files. But the only way it could cope with more pressing requests was to reinforce the manual backup system by producing index cards containing some basic information for each client or establishment. In short a batch-based system with a limited range of data might be useful for managers and researchers, but had little to offer for social workers.

A retrospective comment by the head of the Social Services research section (Ward, 1981) looked at these weaknesses, and put particular emphasis on delays and inaccuracies. The process of entering data, requiring its transfer from area centre to division to HQ, and backwards and forwards again for correction, resulted in some short events (like a two-week admission to a residential setting) becoming history before the computer got hold of them. Further, the number of hands that the data passed through left scope for losses and faults to creep in. On the basis of experience Ward concluded that 'there had to be a delay of at least two months before reasonably accurate information could be produced for any given time period' (Ward, 1981, p. 14). Two important changes were mooted. While some tasks would continue to use the batch approach (annual returns and research, for example), it was essential that a more immediate and direct system be implemented. First it was recommended that the Social Services set up direct links with the computer through terminals (cutting out the middle men), and, second, parts of the service should become interactive and quick (in short go 'on-line').

Going on-line

The view from outside suggests that the decision to go on-line caused some soul-searching. In the first place it involved admitting that a few of the enthusiastic expectations of the original scheme had not wholly come to fruition, though some of this could reasonably be transformed into a recognition of new ideas and technical possibilities for further developments. In addition the Social Services would, for the first time, cease to be solely tenants of computer equipment, and enter into capital expenditure.

The initial proposal (W. Evans, April 1979) envisaged a limited move. Action notes and the already freshly instituted weekly returns would still be sent as before from the front line to divisions. The first visible signs of a new system would be found at divisional HQ, where instead of manually transcribing data on to input forms there would be a keyboard and screen (a terminal) from which direct entries could be made to the computer. The procedure for these entries would allow corrections to be made on the spot. Entries were not then held up at Winchester, but immediately would become part of the computer files. Similarly requests for information could also be made and quickly supplied through the terminals, so it would no longer be necessary for the computer service to circulate index cards for use with urgent tasks. It would follow that all tasks which were previously held up while corrected data were filed, including statistical tables and annual returns, could be speeded up. However, the initial plan did not envisage a wider use of the system (terminals would only be placed in the county headquarters at Winchester, and in the divisional offices, where previously there had been card indexes) or additions to the content of the files.

At this point, in 1979, a policy decision was taken which with hindsight can be seen as central to future developments, although there was hesitation because it was not at all clear if the resources would be made available to meet the demand for computing which was expected to result. It was decided not to treat the process of going on-line as an internal matter for the technical and managerial group, but to invite comments from the department as a whole. The first round of comments and suggestions were issued as a discussion document in August 1979, and these promptly advanced a number of arguments for changes and expansions to the system. Some proposed alterations to the way the information was received and dispensed which would make it more helpful and approachable ('user-friendly'). Others argued for increases to the coverage of the existing files, to offer more information on clients or establishments; while yet more wanted new subject areas to be included in new files, such as information about local voluntary services.

Consultation was followed by a series of seminars to explain and discuss the computer scheme, and a further paper was written in the research section (W. Evans, November 1979) giving a question and answer report on the seminars. Again pressure was observed to extend the system, and this led the Computer Development Group to draw attention to budgetary implications as well as the need for 'a firm commitment from this Department' (W. Evans, November 1979). The list of staff attending the seminars indicated the growing interest in computing, whatever the motivation. Of the 155 participants very few were basic grade social workers, but 61 were staff based in area centres. It was the thin end of the wedge.

The system finally went on-line at the end of 1980. In one important aspect the suggestions from the field were accepted. The contents structure of client files was substantially changed to allow a new range of information to be incorporated at a later date, if and when the network was extended to front-line venues. Files were also made more realistic from the viewpoint of practitioners – for example, the files on establishments now said how many places were actually available, rather than just giving the nominal capacity. The scene was set to draw in social workers, and offer them an information system which they could find useful. At this stage, however, terminals were only fitted in HQ and the divisions. Social workers would have to wait, and a potentially more difficult problem – of access for the Emergency Duty Team – came to the surface. The computer was in the Country Treasurer's Department, and manned twenty-four hours a day for five days a week only.

From MIS to SWIS

Two factors gave a shove to the expansion of the Management

Information System (MIS) into something nearer to a social work information system (SWIS). One was a decision by the county to take the next step of departmental integration in the Social Services and abolish the divisions. This forced the issue of whether direct computer links to Southampton and Portsmouth should remain, and more importantly, of the type of links which HQ would establish with areas. In the same context a Chief Executive's Working Party decisively tipped the scales by recommending that Social Services make maximum use of new technology to manage the accountability of areas, once the ending of divisions exposed the elongated lines of communication.

Social Services' first action was to set up DISP, the Documentation and Information Systems Panel, to initiate the next round of changes. With DISP went DISPatch, started in 1982 as a newsletter for staff of the department. By spring 1983 DISP felt swamped by the pace of computer developments, and established a range of sub-groups to cover:

Personal computing
Specifying a future Management Information System
Monitoring the Management Information System
Non-computer records
Documentation – adults
Documentation – children

From a social worker's viewpoint the interesting groups are likely to be those concerned with personal computing and documentation. The former acknowledges the prospect of expanding computing capacity (in most cases through micro-computers) to area centres and other localised settings. The documentation groups are involved in selecting the range of computer-based data for all departmental uses, and a term of reference is 'To ensure that documentation is appropriately designed to meet both operational and administrative requirements. . . .' (Circular from the Director, 35/83).

It is too early (this is being written in the summer of 1984) to evaluate the work of these groups, or the success of the overall scheme. The new system is not yet fully operational, although large parts of it are running. The facts of expansion sound impressive. Between 1980 and 1984 the county as a whole established over 300 on-line terminal links with its computer. Over fifty of these are in the Social Services, in HQ and all the main area offices (two each). Some outposted HQ staff still do not have terminal access, nor do social workers in hospitals, where six teams will eventually be linked.

Terminal users contribute to and draw on a set of establishments files, broadly as described earlier, and three types of client file. The briefest contains minimal ('index') entries, and is for one-off referrals which did not develop into anything more substantial. Rather more data are available about cases which have been allocated to a social worker, and perhaps received some counselling, but no other services or resources. The most detailed are those which made up the original client files, and are cases to which resources have been committed. By mid-1984 the number of client files stood at about 280 000, six times the number in the original system. Information from social workers in the health services is the largest remaining gap, and it is expected that the total size will approach 3000 000, or about a fifth of the total population of Hampshire. Projections from earlier activities suggest that there will be about 60 000 changes to files each year, a third being new records and the remainder revisions or closures.

Despite the massive amount of information now gathered, the research staff clearly expect that it will settle into a stable and accurate system. In contrast they anticipate quite a lot of inaccuracies as part of the teething difficulties. While these are in part a result of wrong entries being made, confusions and errors have been traced to the process of transferring material from one system to another. This is a sensitive issue at present, because in many area centres the computer has gained a reputation for being error-prone.

For a social worker using a terminal to look at information about a client, there are a maximum of eleven pages or screen displays. Two of them are action rather than information pages, one to open a file, the other to close it. Of the nine information pages, the first contains basic data (the card index equivalent), and is the minimum held about any referral. The next contains some other useful items of information, addresses for example, and is followed by 'referral information', which categorises the initial assessment (referrer, presenting request, primary problem and so forth) and notes the type of allocation. Two pages itemise all resources allocated to the client, and two more similarly cover aids. The remaining pages provide some caseload information and a note of client contacts, both with the social worker and others, including useful contacts outside Social Services.

Introductory courses are given to potential computer users, and it is not difficult to handle the system, whether for immediate interactive information or to use the terminal to request a batch job. The files themselves offer a range of useful information, and the system is now adept at giving the result of a quick search to see if a particular person is known to the department, or if a particular resource or establishment is likely to be available. Yet there are two negative aspects from a social worker's point of view. The system is still not very comfortable to approach. A user needs the help of two manuals, for coding and procedures (though some 'help' is also on offer through the terminal), and most of the material is in coded form. The system has none of the attractiveness of some modern micro-computer programs, and remains essentially a design for the computer-wise rather than the social worker who wants to use it without inconvenience. It still looks like a system with its feet embedded in old-style programming techniques for statistical analysis, rather than something with, for example, the panache in presentation of a good word-processor program.

The other practice disadvantage is that despite the increased range of data on file, there is no realistic prospect that it could hold enough information or have the flexibility to substitute for traditional client folders on active cases. So while a strong and effective move has been made to involve social workers and offer them a useful computer service, there is still a very long way to go. The Hampshire experience, where there has been dependable managerial commitment, as well as continuous creative effort from the research section, indicates that the transition phase will be lengthy. During this time social workers will be faced with a hybrid information system, part on computer and part (their case-files) in folders.

For some social workers in Hampshire there is as yet no duality because there is no computer link. These are (temporarily) from the big hospitals, and (more permanently) small sub-offices or outposted settings. The cost of installing terminals for these would be high, and Hampshire's solution is to have the outline parts of both client and establishment files put on to microfiche, with a weekly replacement of an updated set. Small bases are then provided with microfiche reader. A careful process exists for issuing and recovering microfiche slides, but this is accepted as a risky area, and consequently kept under close scrutiny.

Security and the Code of Practice

The Hampshire system has grown up with a preoccupation for security, which is far from unusual. Most computer systems in social services departments have built-in security barriers. The wider aspects of security are taken up in Chapter 6, where it will be suggested that the real risks are not of an accident or breakdown of the system (though on exceedingly rare occasions that is possible), but of intentional breaches. Here the security arrangements set into the Hampshire system will be described.

The first part of any security framework is to control access to the computer equipment itself, and this is covered both by the normal locking-up arrangements for the social work offices and by the closure of the computer at some vulnerable times (such as at weekends when the office is empty). The next stage is to identify and authorise the users, which is done by a two-part process. Every authorised user's name must be registered with the computer, so that when a user types it on the terminal as part of the procedure for getting access, the computer can recognise and accept it. That part would not be too hard to breach, simply by trying out a few common names in the reasonable expectation that the computer would 'recognise' one of them. The next part, however, is to type in a secret password, selected by the user during the original authorisation process, and known only to the user and the computer. An authorised user is encouraged to change password at regular intervals. Someone trying to get access by experimenting with different names and passwords is cut off after a few unsuccessful tries, and the computer records from which terminal these attempts came.

Once a user has gained access, two different forms of entry come into operation. Minimum use is 'read only', which means that information can be received from the computer, but no files can be introduced, altered or deleted. The more powerful access is 'read and amend', and while all social worker users would expect a 'read only' authorisation, usually only one person (probably a senior clerical officer) in each office can 'amend'. The computer notes all attempts to change files, so these can be traced back if anything odd occurs. To avoid accidental (or malicious!) deleting, all deleted files are not destroyed, but transferred to an archive. In the long term some total deletion will have to be considered, for political and ethical reasons if nothing else, but that has not yet been faced.

Two further user limitations are possible, one to restrict the range of files which a particular user can see, and the other requiring personal collection for anyone who wants a print of an entry rather than a screen display.

Even with these controls there will still be a lot of authorised users in a large social services department, so a great deal depends on the standard of behaviour these people adopt. An authorised user can easily become a misuser. The Social Services has issued a Code of Practice (and acknowledges a debt to the local Health Authority for some of it). This goes through the system in some detail, explaining its uses, and spelling out specific misuses. Attached to it is a set of Security Rules, making the obvious practical points which will be familiar to all holders of credit cards. Every user is then required to sign an undertaking that the Code of Practice and Security Rules have been read and understood, and will be observed. A separate Code and undertaking applies to anyone wanting printed information, though in any event this must have prior approval from HQ.

Misuse, or, in the terms of the Code, 'disallowed purposes', takes two forms. There is a general statement defining as disallowed anything not specifically allowed in the Code or approved by the Director. Then there is a specific assertion that 'No access to and use of data is allowed where exploitation by commercial or industrial organisations could occur' (Code of Practice, para. 4).

A more complex section concerns 'indirect users'. The problem is not composite statistical information, but personal data about clients, presumably collected under the auspices of professional confidentiality. Depending on the seniority of the member of staff giving authorisation this can, in some circumstances, be handed out to other departments of the local authority, other social services departments or welfare agencies, or external organisations for research purposes. The intention is quite clearly to conform to traditional practices of sharing information (in case conferences, for example), but it looks more controversial and open to abuse when written out. It is a practice which social workers might prefer not to see formally acknowledged.

Comment

As was stated in the Introduction, Hampshire's system has not been described because it is necessarily the most modern in a social services department. Some others have established more comprehensive files, or moved further into the new dimension of personal computing. Yet Hampshire does offer some lessons gained from experience, and some guidelines to good practice. The difficulties tend to have centred around the task of getting a computer system set up or expanded without causing too much confusion or creating too many inaccuracies. The lesson from this may have to do with the value of gradual, step-by-step implementation, though even here the reality of teething troubles has to be faced. A further lesson is clearly that an 'off-line' system has very limited uses, and many disadvantages. A harder experience to evaluate is the continuing use of a computer belonging to another department, rather than becoming more 'purpose designed'. This may have been the only way, of course, given the history of financial stringency.

There are several guidelines to good practice. The Social Services have enjoyed a continuity of managerial commitment to the development of the system, as well as continuity in certain vital personnel to carry it through. The system, despite earlier criticism of its appearance, is logical, coherent and fast becoming comprehensive for all purposes except for details of client–worker interactions. It has moved away from a selective approach, and hence overcome the risks of distortion in a system where part of the agency information is on the computer and available for staff, while part is off and less easily accessible. The system has blossomed simultaneously with the decision to involve front-line staff in its planning. This may not be cause and effect, but the creative stimulus of wide discussion is very apparent to the outsider. The particular arrangement of consultation and planning, via DISP and its sub-groups, is a framework for continuing development. Some social services departments have opted to implement a computer system following the commissioned report of an outside consultant, and this carries risks of a scheme which shows insufficient knowledge of the agency's way of running, and does not command staff support. Hampshire's approach has had the opposite impact, and generated a lot of commitment from principal area officers and other senior staff. Future policy is aimed to avoid computer developments being distinct from other activities, and instead to see them as an integrated part of overall agency plans. Finally, although the Social Services has created a massive client file, and thereby raised all the fundamental issues about data banks, its organisational response to security, through the Security Rules and Code of Practice, reflect a thoroughly practical attempt to minimise risks of abuse.

4

Computers in Social Work Practice

The previous chapter described the computer system of one social services department. It was called a 'Management Information System', and in its early phase operated as such; but it gradually expanded its accessibility so that it became physically available to social workers, and at the same time began to offer useful functions for front-line staff. This chapter looks further at computer uses among social workers and others in direct contact with clients. It excludes future uses (which are considered in Chapter 8) and confines itself to schemes already in operation, albeit in some cases experimentally. One assumption made in this chapter is that if a function is available to social workers the equipment needed to take advantage of it is also there and usable. In practice this is not always the case, especially where the agency is dependent on sharing someone else's computer. In Hampshire, for example, the files are not available at weekends to the emergency duty staff because the computer is closed down. In most local authorities outposted and sub-office workers are unlikely to be able to use a computer or terminal without the inconvenience of travelling to it. It is an important difference between management and front-line staff that the latter tend to be much more dispersed. Indeed, the developing policy of 'community social work' could well have the result of spreading practitioners into still smaller clusters. Put another way, there would be considerable capital cost in giving all social workers the same ease of access as managers, and where a piece of equipment is only likely to be used for a tiny part of its capacity, the cost may not be justifiable. This raises issues which will be taken up in Chapter 7. For the present access is taken for granted.

The history of computers in social work practice is more recent and more complex than developments in management. Social service managers have always had the advantage of sharing needs with colleagues in other settings, and this has given great impetus to computerised management systems. Social work does share needs with some other groups (doctors, for example), but there is not an extensive linking of social workers and others into the sort of large coherent potential user-group which would command attention from computer system designers. Social work applications have, therefore, tended to emerge in a more fragmented and segmented way, with a much bigger role for locally produced experiments and individual efforts. As a result of starting out at a later stage relative to technical developments, many social work computer pioneers have designed with micro-computers in mind. Indeed social work practice applications may well not need the large capacity of a mainframe system, and the home computer or small office machine is cheaper. In a wider sense the economic factor might have become important if there had been a major thrust in computerised practice schemes, but the small range of developments has limited the pressure placed on budgets for computer purchases.

While starting later has given some advantages, in the bigger range of equipment available, and perhaps the greater familiarity with computing, there have been disadvantages. Within the social services computing has tended to be seen at times as the province of the managers, and as will be argued in Chapter 6 there is a view of computing as a tool of control. Hence some of the 'approved' efforts to develop practice programs have come as carefully considered arms to existing management systems. This is not necessarily a helpful jumping off point, and 'there has not been complete user satisfaction with the operation of these multipurpose systems' (Chapman, 1976, p. 5).

A further significant difference in the experiences of managers and practitioners has been the absence, for the latter, of any events comparable in their impact to the formation of social services departments and then local government reorganisation. Both of these presented managers with an increase in the scale of agency activities of such dimensions that many (especially in the bigger departments) could see computing as the only way to cope. Nothing has been done to social workers to direct their attention so explicitly towards new technologies.

Much the most persistent contrast over the last decade, however, has been in attitudes towards computer uses. For managers any political and ethical dilemmas have been strongly countered by the knowledge that computers had a clear and undeniable value in aiding the management task. There has been no such certainty for practitioners. Useful applications to social work practice would need arguing and demonstrating, and if there is a prima facie case it is against rather than for computing – in that the idea of using a computer in work with clients does seem to interfere in the worker–client relationship, and to make impersonal what is one of the most personal of jobs. In consequence computing has not had a smooth passage among social workers, who have both exposed the difficulty of incorporating such activity into the social work task, and paid greater attention to wider issues, especially concerning confidentiality and client rights. In the view of some (for example, Tutt, 1983), social workers have used these genuine concerns as grounds for digging in their toes, and taking on a more comprehensive resistance to computers.

The core argument among managers for using computers was a simple one: 'we have a problem: computer technology offers a solution: let's get together'. In social work practice the arguments have had to be more sophisticated. Hoshino suggests that social workers must accept the implications of 'the emergence of "the personal social services" as a distinct and increasingly important system of social welfare, one in which the social work profession plays a pivotal role' (Hoshino, 1982, p. 5). The implication he wishes to see acknowledged is, in general terms, the need for efficiency, with computers as necessary aids. He links this argument to the observation that social workers will be letting down their colleagues in other service professions (in law, medicine and education) if the computer is ignored.

Other points have nudged social workers in the same direction, either explicitly or by implication. Rees, for example, discusses the element of irrationality in the way caseloads are handled, noting the impact of the personal preferences of social workers on the allocation of clients, and the difficulties of coping with workload management while under pressure. He concludes that in some circumstances 'social workers felt that the responsibility for finding remedies was not theirs', while, when facing 'problems of people in whom they were very interested, they used their time creatively and worked at producing solutions even though none seems obvious' (Rees, 1978, p. 104). What he is doing is posing a major question-mark over the objectivity and efficiency of workload management at the level of front-line teams, and implying the need for something more rational, or at least for recognition of the irrationality. Payne, in a study of area teams, takes up a similar theme, when discussing the importance of improving skills in information management (Payne, 1979). He draws attention to reports on social work tragedies, in which social services departments are criticised for an inadequate exploration of basic information. While this is just one aspect of workload management, the problem appears to span more widely. Stevenson notes this, and offers pointers to a solution:

> there is clear evidence that many social workers have not found ways of 'managing' their work in the face of competing and conflicting demands and uncertainties about goals. What seems to be needed, therefore, is support which combines the subtler aspects of professional development, including awareness of the part one's feelings and attitudes play in the way caseloads are 'managed' with more formal methods. . . . (HMSO, 1978, para. 13.23).

The idea of establishing a balanced mixture in social work practice of professional judgement and a dependable structured framework is one approach to handling a caseload efficiently. The role for the computer becomes to aid the functioning of the 'dependable structured framework', a task which involves helping to iron out the eccentricities of professional judgement, plug gaps left by fallible human memories, and contribute to a balanced overview of the workload. The argument clearly stops short of interfering with social work performances, aiming primarily at using computers to make the work, both of individual and team, more effective.

If the computer can aid effectiveness, can it make a further contribution by saving time on some tasks? The prospect that a positive answer can be given forms another part of the overall argument. The social worker's job is made up of a diverse mixture of activities, ranging from direct face-to-face meetings with clients, through to a cluster of repetitive 'office' chores. The computer, in so far as it offers a more mechanised and streamlined approach, can help reduce the time spent on the mundane, and release the social worker to do the 'real' job.

Social workers have an information base in the case-file, and they give much attention to recording, reviewing, revising, updating, assessing, prognosticating and drawing conclusions from this file. Each client is unique, and each case-file will therefore be different in content to all others. But it is just as predictably similar in structure to others. The same contrast can be made about social work practice. The process of social work requires the worker to establish some sort of relationship with the client, which in turn serves the purpose of helping to clarify a predicament and suggest ways of handling it. The circumstances of the client will be unique, as will be the precise nature of the relationship which the social worker establishes. Yet the predicament is likely to be one which that worker, or the worker's team, has met before, and the procedures adopted may derive from a form of approach (a precedent, a well-used theory or just plain habit) which has also been employed on many previous occasions. All that is being argued here is that our traditional commitment to the uniqueness of the client and the client–worker relationship represents a generalisation which can usefully be analysed to establish exactly what is and is not unique. The moment it becomes possible to accept the utility of such approaches as comparing like with like, or looking back to see what was done in similar circumstances in the past, or checking what seems to have worked and not worked when the same sort of problem has been encountered before, then a role has been found for the computer.

These, then, are some of the arguments which have been advanced to give a little forward shove to computing in social work practice. What, in practical terms, has actually happened? The rest of this chapter will seek an answer, and will separate the response into three sections. These will look, in turn, at the extension into practice of centralised information systems, the use of computers for functions involving calculations, like benefits entitlements, and finally computer uses in assessment and treatment.

Information systems and practice

In the previous chapter, and indeed through most of the book so far, computing in the personal social services is equated with the use of an information system, to store, present and analyse the agency's supply of data. The emphasis is on the files, client and resource, and on the speed with which they can be shuffled around to produce individual and composite information. Social services managers seem to have been content to promote a comprehensive and efficient system of this type because it meets most of their needs. For social workers also there is a lot to be gained from an information system, but its value is limited. The point has already been made that a centralised computer filing scheme would have difficulty incorporating the minutiae of case-files, so forcing social workers either to accept the inconvenience of a dual computer-manual system, or to make a radical reappraisal of the part recording plays in social work (worth thinking about?). If the computer files are not on-line they have little to offer front-line staff, whatever their contents, though there may be uses for locally based managers.

What then has been set up so far for social workers through information systems? The LAMSAC survey (LAMSAC, 1982) suggested that applications to date only constituted comprehensive information systems in a minority of cases, while the majority showed quite a variety in the segments of data on computer file. Child-care and boarding-out records were the most popular, followed by care registers for specific client groups. Home-help provision and services offered through the Chronically Sick and Disabled Persons Act had also been put on computer by some authorities. LAMSAC found that the future plans of many social services departments included extending into more comprehensive client-record systems, and in the time since the survey it is reasonable to assume that this has occurred. The survey is less clear about the comprehensiveness of resource files, but it is highly likely that client records will include all allocations of aids and services.

An accessible on-line system has several specific uses for social workers. In many social services departments it is now possible, when a person is referred to an area team (less often if the referral is directed somewhere else), to find out if the agency has had any previous contact. When there has been contact the office where it occurred would be identified, and any social worker to whom the case was allocated. In most instances an outline history of contacts would be kept, listing also when and what resources the client had received. A status record would indicate whether the existing file was open or closed, and possibly the name of any person or office to be contacted in the event of a re-referral.

In addition to basic factual information, any system which identifies particular risk factors (of child abuse, for example) will draw attention to them. It should also be able to point to aliases and linked files (such as for other members of the same family), and to call up the names of possibly useful people, such as the GP. If a voluntary agency has been involved, or some particular person has taken an interest, this will be available.

In short, a reasonable central information system will provide a helpful summary of facts, some bits of background material, known risks, people to contact and services already provided. In a comprehensive system it is safe to assume that if the person is not on the computer file then it is a new referral, though many agencies have not yet got themselves set up to ensure this with certainty. Furthermore, the on-line system makes it possible to get this material very quickly, at the time the referral is received, and usually (out-of-hours referrals are the most frequent exception) before any action has to be taken. All of this is an important advance on manual systems, which are usually confined to data on the limited number of files held in the local office. At the same time there is the important limitation of a lack of depth in the computer file, and usually the complete absence of any qualitative material, such as would aid counselling. If a client is known elsewhere the social worker is forced into the cumbersome task of chasing up staff and files from another office, or doing without a conventional case-history, or starting a new one.

Computer files of agency resources are usually set up to contain descriptive information about residential and day-care facilities in the agency, which in many instances extends to include a range of other data, on foster parents, voluntary services, private facilities and so forth. The emphasis is very much on tangible resources, places where it may be possible for a client to go, for a day, week or life. Sometimes the information goes a bit further, to identify what aids are available, and from where. The type of information sets the parameters of the resource: what it does, what sort of users it takes, age and sex, catchment area, number of places, charges, dates, durations – the sort of preliminary material a social worker needs, but which those who have been around for a while will already have in their heads.

These kinds of files are much more likely to be created so that the agency can run off annual returns or quick counts of day-care places for elderly mentally confused ex-managers, than to help a social worker in this descriptive sense (except of course the new worker). Resource files only start to become useful when they take on one or both of two characteristics, and these have become available in some agencies. One is the extension of the information on file to the point where it includes material that is not routinely in a social worker's head. This may mean real depth of local data, or moving into regional and national resources. In practice social services departments are not keen to offer information which might incite staff to press for costly out-of-area resources, so local information has had more attention. For example, Whaley (1983) has pioneered a Community Information Directory for the Caradon Area of Cornwall Social Services Department, which already contains entries of approaching 800 resources. The data can be searched as a body, or segmented into different categories of resource, or parish in which it is available. Whaley, who is a field social worker, developed this file under the impetus of 'personal frustration at finding such information when requiring it and . . . my inability to organise such information in a personal collection or an efficient manual office system' (p. 24).

The other extension of resource files which has shown itself to be of real value to social workers concerns the recording of currently available facilities, in terms of vacancies in residential or day-care settings, in IT groups (whatever IT means to you!), of foster parents or other scarce provisions. Some resources are in such demand that at the first sniff of a vacancy social workers descend like vultures to snap it up, and any attempt to put it on a computer file would inevitably be retrospective. As a result some agencies are trying to introduce a sense of order and rationality to the allocation of scarce facilities, by making sure that competing demands for them are properly balanced through such as a formal allocation meeting. To make this work, all those staff who might

want to request a resource for a client have to be given
information about vacancies, on a time scale which gives them the
opportunity to apply. This can be part of the information related
to specific resources on a computer file, or as part of a changing
list of 'current vacancies'.

In some resource files there is, additionally or alternatively, a
more broadly based scope to survey available resources, to aid a
social worker who is wanting to review a range of possibilities for
a client. These data can include a note of waiting lists, where they
are kept, or an indication of when and how frequently facilities of
various types come up. However, this is edging near to the limits
of current experiments and into future developments.

In client and resource files some flexible space can be reserved
for random non-standardised entries, in the sense that what goes
into these spaces is unique to each client or resource (i.e. it is not
designed for composite analysis). This is a long way from
accommodating a lot of detail, but it permits the brief qualitative
or even evaluative comment – like the ability to note on the file of
an old people's home that it is 'Good with grumpy men' – literally
just a few words. The Hampshire system can offer this, as can
some of the more widely available schemes like SOSCIS and
PROBIS.

There are just a few developments which are extending the
managerial output of the information system in a helpful way for
social workers. This primarily involves making the conventional
annual returns and statistical analyses available for each area or
work team separately. The local team is therefore offered much
the same data-base for the management of its own workload as
senior managers have for the whole agency. The value for social
workers is that it gives them a basis for scrutinising and
responding to directives from above, and making a contribution
to the negotiations which lead to policy and executive decisions.

The extension and refinement of information systems in
personal social service agencies is a continuing process, and in
some areas the change is fast. If social workers are to get good
value in the near future the reader will need to be able to comment,
with accuracy, that the last few pages have been overtaken by
events. Developments of existing systems are more likely to have
positive spin-offs for social workers than negative ones, and the
faster the change the more the practitioner is likely to benefit,

because change will involve moving outwards from a narrow managerial preoccupation. Estimating the next few years is not easy. The LAMSAC survey is pessimistic, noting that two items of particular interest to practitioners, information directories and area records, came at the bottom of a priority scale in the context of general support for the development of a computer package for social services departments (LAMSAC, 1982, para. 6). On the other hand the pace of technological development creates a certain impetus to dash along and keep in touch.

Computers as calculators

There are a number of tasks undertaken by social workers which require calculations to be made of a precise kind. This may be to work out an elderly person's eligibility for a residential home, or who is the 'nearest relative' for the purposes of a compulsory admission under the 1983 Mental Health Act, or the sequence of events to be followed in observing the boarding-out regulations. What characterises all of these is that they have a mechanistic component, of working out a score or following a fixed path; they are unvarying repetitive processes, and social workers have to go through some of them quite frequently. Much the most complex and frequently needed process of this kind involves helping clients assess their potential eligibility or check their actual assessment for welfare benefits.

Several computer systems for welfare benefits assessment are under development or on trial, though at present there is no fully operational problem-free version which is also comprehensive. They have proved harder to develop in practice than their designers anticipated. Most are designed to use on micro-computers, but several social services departments are planning terminal-to-mainframe schemes.

The social security provisions of the UK are so complicated that any method of working out individual entitlements is likely to be error-prone. Many DHSS assessments, just like Inland Revenue tax assessments, are regularly successfully challenged. No computer scheme can be put on a pedestal and operate perfectly in this sector, but Whaley (1983, p. 14) suggests four advantages of computing:

1. Although it may take a long time to obtain and feed into the computer all the information it needs before making an assessment, the calculation itself can be done rapidly and immediately.

2. No errors of calculation. This, however, may be a simplistic view, for though the computer will calculate correctly, it will use the data it is fed by the claimant and the calculation formula given by the programmer. These are the places where mistakes are likely.

3. The highest optimum level of benefit can be calculated, by taking into account possible choices in the way an assessment is handled.

4. A printed version of the data fed in and the calculations made can be provided, and this is useful for comparing with the official assessment, and as a basis for appeal.

Two computer systems for calculating welfare-benefit entitlements have by now received long trials, and acted as pioneers for a blossoming of developments. Both aim to be comprehensive in the benefits covered, so include central government and local authority provisions – family income supplement, supplementary benefit, disability benefits and health service prescription exemptions, as well as rent and rate rebates, free school meals and other educational benefits. The system designed by Nigel Murray of Surrey University was tried out in Brighton before being taken over by DHSS for a more extensive trial. It is set up for direct use by a potential claimant, unaided. Gareth Morgan's version, initially at the Llanrumney (Cardiff) Citizens' Advice Bureau, and later at other CABx, involves the claimant passing material to a member of staff, who then puts it into the computer. The process for the user, in both of these and all subsequent systems, is for the user to answer a large number of questions, many of an intimate personal nature, and some needing information to be brought along to the session (on precise earnings over the last few months for the family, for example). This can take anything up to an hour to enter through the computer's keyboard, and then a calculation is offered, with a printed copy.

The experiments were not totally successful, and although they took place in 1982, we still await a definitive welfare benefits programme. Hence there have been numerous further trials of different systems, but none have gained a solid foothold. There are several problems. The most apparent one for the potential claimant is that however 'user-friendly' the computers try to be they come across as asking interminable and sometimes plain stupid questions. Lynes, in a review of the two early systems, comments: 'The main requirement is stamina. I watched a disabled single man patiently working through questions such as 'Do you suffer from ulcerative colitis?'' but finally losing patience when asked to declare his income from child-minding.' (Lynes, 1982, p. 424.) The trouble is that computers cannot adapt themselves, as a human interviewer can, to the person sitting at the keyboard; so all questions have to be asked and answered, however irrelevent they may be, and there is no way of discriminating, so that questions can be acknowledged as particularly intrusive, or pointless but unavoidable. Even so a study of 398 people who tried the DHSS experiment suggested that a substantial majority (85 per cent) preferred a computer to a DHSS officer, while fewer (58 per cent) would rather have benefits assessed by the machine than by a social worker. The main reason for the preference was that the computer did not keep people waiting for attention (Ebstein, 1984).

Other weaknesses are less visible, but in some ways more serious because they affect the accuracy and relevance of the calculation. The real difficulties for the computer, especially with supplementary benefit, stem from discretion and the definition of terms. The official with the power to grant a benefit may well have some limited range of choice, and will also have to decide whether the circumstances of a particular application meet the criteria for eligibility, in a context in which the criteria are not themselves precise. Social workers will know of many instances (with attendance allowances, for example) when the facts look to justify a benefit, but it has been refused. Computers like to calculate on certainties, and have great difficulty coping with tentative data or a hazy basis for making a calculation. It is no help to a claimant to be told 'You may qualify for a benefit, but then again you may not'.

Local variations in benefits can also be troublesome, and any welfare benefits package developed for widespread use will need a running-in phase to accommodate to local authority practices as well as any possibilities from local voluntary and charitable sources.

All of these problems showed up in early trials, and more recent developments have tried to overcome them by a less ambitious set of aims. This has involved either being less comprehensive, and instead concentrating on specific benefits, or moving away from the idea of precise calculation towards a more tentative approach. The former can be useful in relation to isolated benefits, or where the claimant has a possible choice of which benefit to seek, and wants guidance on the best approach. Its big weakness is that it can no longer claim to offer an overall comment on benefits eligibility. The alternative approach (which was anticipated in the DHSS trial) leads either to a slight adjustment in language (you 'may' rather than you 'do' qualify for a benefit) while retaining an estimate of the amount, or to the abandonment of the calculation of the precise benefit, and simply a suggestion that it might be worth applying for such and such benefits.

Efforts are continuing to find an acceptable system, and also to see what can be done with low-cost equipment, especially the readily available home computers. A recent package of this kind which provoked DHSS interest has been written by Professor Jarman of the St Mary's Hospital Medical School, on the justification that so many patients visiting general practitioners 'were under stress because they were hard up – single parents, some of the elderly, people like that' (*The Times*, 14 May 1984). The need for an effective benefits assessment package is widespread and pressing, but it has proved surprisingly difficult to deliver. The Greater London Council has sponsored a newsletter (*Computanews*) to circulate the latest information about developments.

There is a sting in the tail. However successful a computer program may be at making accurate assessments, it is not in itself a solution 'to the problem of low take up any more than means testing is a solution to the problem of poverty' (Adler and du Feu, 1977, p. 445). That may be something of an overstatement, particularly if a home computer program can be made widely available and run in privacy; but it does counter the dubious claim in the review of Jarman's system that: 'If widely adopted, it could lead to many more claims.' (*The Times*, 14 March 1984.) Lynes, a veteran welfare rights campaigner, is both cautious: 'This is a field in which white elephants can be expensive' – and sceptical, in view of 'the advantage human beings have over computers when it comes to sorting out misunderstandings. Computers may be all right for dating, but they'd be hopeless at marriage guidance.' (Lynes, 1982, p. 424.)

Computers in client assessment and treatment

This will be a sketchy section for the simple reason that there is not a great deal to report from current practice, and a more coherent analysis of what should be possible will be held over to Chapter 8. It is likely, particularly in the US, that many programs are at present being written and tried out, but few have been described for a wider audience. The explosion is happening, but few of the bits have yet fallen to earth for the student to pick up and analyse.

The first developments have been in using the computer as an aid to assessment processes. This has tended to take one of two forms. Hoshino notes that in the US some agencies 'have developed systems in which workers directly enter data on clients through terminals and retrieve information for such porposes as preparing court reports and child placements' (Hoshino, 1982, p. 8.) The extension of the scope of information stores to make detailed case material available has already been discussed, with the conclusion that in this country the initial structuring of such systems for managerial functions has been an inhibitor. In general, therefore, only the bare bones of factual data could currently be obtained from a computer for use in a report or assessment of an individual client, and this is probably not worth the effort of the social worker. If the worker has to go through a conventional file for some material, why not get it all from this source? The issue is one of comprehensiveness, and a computer wil come into its own when all the recorded data for a report can be got from it, and better still when they can be copied straight into the report in the place and format indicated by the social worker.

Some modern information systems are beginning to get near to this potential. There are two needs. One, already discussed, is the ability to store detail on the computer (i.e. the equivalent of a conventional case-file). The other is the ability to be able to retrieve that data in a clear and readable way (not in some form of obscure coding), and then link them to the abilities of such as a word-processor for slotting bits of data or whole paragraphs into the right position of a report. Systems like PROBIS look as though they could well have this scope, for extending to take on more detail and for linking (the jargon phrase is 'export–import') the data-base to a good presentation program, like one for word-processing. PROBIS is appropriate to mention here because it is designed for the Probation Service, and that service in turn uses a form of report which is particularly suitable for computing. The point about social inquiry reports for the Court is that while they do not have the rigidity of filling in a form, they do need to contain some basic factual material and do have broad standardisation in structure, length and type of content. Computers love standardisation.

Computers are also fast, and another use in assessment is where their speed facilitates an otherwise difficult task. Social workers will have regular experience of circumstances in which they are forced to make a skimpy assessment (especially the initial one of a new referral) when they are fully aware that there is much more detail and complexity to unearth, given time. Pressures of work and shortage of staff time lead to half-informed guesses rather than well-documented decisions, and some of the more difficult forms of assessment may have to be put aside altogether. An illustration of this is the difficult social/psychological/medical task with an elderly client of deciding whether a particular form of behaviour reflects depression or the onset of dementia. The symptoms can be similar, but the treatment is different, so careful assessment is needed. But the process of assessment is time-consuming and difficult. A micro-computer-aided program has been developed at University College Hospital in London, which both speeds up the process of collecting assessment data and prints an analysis of the findings. Furthermore it is considered to be easier and more acceptable to both staff and client than the previous method (*The Guardian*, 28 June 1984).

Another context in which manual assessment becomes difficult is one in which the worker needs to record a series of observations, of individual, family or group behaviour. A problem here is the practical one of being able to record observations quickly and systematically enough, even with the help of prepared charts. Several computer programs can now cope with this, some of them on small portable micro-computers which can be rested on the lap like a note-pad. Each form of behaviour to be observed is given a code number or letter, and when it begins the observer presses that button on the keyboard. Pressing the button again indicates the end of the behaviour, and as well as printing all the observations the computer can offer an analysis which times the duration of each of them, and puts them in sequence so that they can be considered in conjunction with other events in the same phase.

It should be said that although these developments are relevant to social workers, they are essentially multi-disciplinary efforts, with psychologists and doctors playing a leading role. Members of these two professions perhaps have more routine involvement (and maybe are more comfortable?) with structured processes, of a kind which can more easily be seen in computing terms. A third group, educationalists, need to be acknowledged for their con-tribution to some developments in training processes. These are well-established in general education, and are already becoming widespread in special education, which is the point of overlap for social workers. Leaving aside whether involvement in such things as remedial learning, literacy campaigns or home economics teaching is appropriate for social workers as part of their own task, the availability and usefulness of these computer-aided services opens up the range of treatment opportunities. The contribution the computer can make is in its facility to display information in an attractive and useful way, to go at the learner's pace, and respond to the learner's efforts with praise and encouragement. It is impersonal equipment with a personal touch, offering what Seddon calls an 'electronic handshake if we get it right!' (Seddon, 1983, p. 66).

An aid to treatment which is already offered in some social services departments, and can be as conveniently handled on the centralising large computers as on the small local ones, is a kind of diary reminder service. An obvious application is where law or agency decision requires contact with a client at specified intervals, and the computer can send reminders to a social worker of contacts coming due. An equally easy extension allows the social worker to feed into the computer the data to permit a series of future reminders (appointments, anniversaries and so forth).

As a final point in this chapter it is perhaps appropriate to discuss one controversial aid to decision-making which has its origins well before computers came on the scene. The use of empirical data has long been established in the social sciences as a basis for drawing general conclusions and making inferences about trends. The data stored in computer information systems constitute the empirical base, and is already widely used in management to aid projections of future service and resource needs. In some areas it is also making a contribution to more localised planning of how resources are deployed and social workers' time used. The more controversial aspect is the use of this material not just to project composite future circumstances, but predict outcomes and 'best' services in individual cases. There is a long history to work on prediction (Trasler, 1960; Parker, 1966), and grounds for taking it seriously, but its use with computers brings it into the general argument about the dehumanising impact of modern technology (to be discussed in a later chapter). There is some current use, for example in using computer-stored records of past experiences to aid matching a child to a potential foster parent, but it barely scratches the surface of what is possible.

5

Hands on the Computer

Computing is only just beginning to come into consideration as a subject for the curricula of basic training courses in social work and social servicing, and it follows that many staff of the agencies will have no computing knowledge or experience. However, an increasing number will have encountered a computer in some context, and it is relevant to ask whether these contacts have helped or hindered, encouraged or deterred potential users in the personal social services.

Leaving aside the peripheral aspects – computerised bills and word-processed letters from *Readers' Digest* or the Consumers' Association assuring us that we may have won a fortune – it is television and the home computer which feature most often. For many years the computer in television was confined to the occasional documentary programme and the much more frequent thriller series, in which it represented the technological miracle, incomprehensible but magical, massive and visually stunning, a vital weapon in the fight against international crime. The more adventurous ones had a mind and will of their own, and a soft voice to convey their messages. There was a snippet of truth in this picture. Early computers were massive, and they did have whirring disks, flashing lights and arrays of control panels. This was the presentation format of the 1960s, but because it has such visual attractions television has tended to keep with it, and this has created a gulf in comprehension between the computer of fiction and the computer of reality.

Regular attention to computing in the media coincided with the upsurge of interest in home computing and the development of computer studies in schools. In this context the computer becomes something quite different – small, rather insignificant to look at, much like a typewriter to use and with less glamour and mystery. While it can be used for serious purposes it is mainly for games, which require speed of thought combined with manual dexterity, and keep the kids quiet for hours on end until the novelty wears off.

The presentation of the more serious side, whether in education or business, tends to serve as a deterrent to those who feel themselves to be 'outsiders'. A part of the computer revolution is the development of a new educational curriculum in schools, which renders obsolete some of the learning of adult generations; just as fundamental have been new forms of business practice. The impact is to make adults, even those who consider themselves to be numerate, feel like outdated, and perhaps soon to be unwanted, members of society. The media adds insult to injury by emphasising the smugness of the computer-wise, their insight, foresight and general superiority.

This is an overstated picture, because it ignores the large numbers who neither know nor care about computers. At the same time it focuses on some of the dilemmas of computer integration into society. In a different context from this book the breadth of the issues could be discussed, with social workers appearing as citizens in a wider community, and as one small cog in the machinery of state. Within the present remit it is sufficient to note the 'image' of the computer as it is presented to social workers, and the problems which arise from it. There is the unreal gap in comprehension between the flashy big machines and the little home computers which creates confusion and denies the reality of technological closeness; then comes the association from the beginning of big computers with militaristic and criminal activities, which serves to pose fundamental political questions about the way these inaccessible machines are used; and there is the persistent suggestion that the lack of computer knowledge implies a major gap in personal capacities, which, coupled to the mysticism described in an earlier chapter, serves to create resentment and distancing. There emerges, for social workers and the rest of us, a practical and psychological polarisation between, on the one hand, the excitement of living through an era of tremendous technological growth, and feeling part of it, and in contrast the insecurity, powerlessness and irritation at being made to feel obsolete and out in the cold. The next chapter looks at the way these broad issues have been interpreted and argued within the personal social services. The remainder of this chapter has the more restricted aim of joining the attitudes and feelings discussed above to a range of practical aspects of being a computer user.

Fear of trying

Conversations with social workers about using computers lead regularly to a couple of comments: 'I can't do it because I'm not numerate' and 'If I used the computer I'd be sure to put a jinx on it.' Both suggest a mixture of personal reluctance and insecurity, lack of knowledge, and a hint at two more substantial arguments for keeping a distance. The fear of being innumerate and therefore a computer duffer is genuine but misplaced, yet it does move towards the important question of what new skills and knowledge a social worker must have in order to become a computer user. The idea of putting a jinx on a piece of equipment may presuppose all sorts of assumptions about personal magnetism or ability to mess things up, or a record of 'incidents', but it may also link up with the observation that computers have not yet established a good record of accuracy and reliability.

The Shorter Oxford Dictionary defines 'compute' as to count or determine by calculation, so it is not surprising that the very label 'computer' conjures up mathematics and the need for a user to be 'good with figures'. The early history of computers reinforced this view to the extent that it has been difficult in the last decade to combat the entrenched prejudice that computers are limited in this way. The author had sporadic contacts with mainframe computers from the late 1960s, and laid hands on a micro in 1977, noting pompously at the time that it helped not just to be and feel numerate, but that training in symbolic logic was also handy. Even if such a remark was valid at the time, it has little relevance today, except to a small group of specialist programmers.

The numeracy view perhaps continues because there is enough understanding around to realise that computers do function arithmetically, regardless of the way they communicate with us. Even worse, they do not function on the conventional decimal system of figures, but in some more mystical way reflected by words like 'Boolean' and 'hex'. The vital point for the social worker to hang on to is that it really is the form of communication which matters and not what goes on inside the computer's guts. Numeracy or mathematical knowledge is relevant only as an aid to some background understanding. It is not essential.

Staying for a while with this background, it may be helpful to know that computers make use of a binary system. Whereas our normal (decimal) system of figures employs ten separate symbols, the binary system uses only two, the digits 0 and 1 (in the jargon binary digits are labelled 'bits'). Most school children can count in binary, but that is not grounds for insecurity. The important point is that because binary contains only the two digits it can be translated into electrical terms as current on – current off. Any decimal number can be expressed in binary and stated within the computer by turning on a current for '1' and turning it off for '0'. Similarly any letter can be given a corresponding code in binary and conveyed in the same way. Virtually all computers handle figures and letters (called alphanumeric'), and many can offer pictures (graphics).

It would be an impossible task for social workers if everything had to be translated into binary code before it could be put into (or received from) the computer, but of course computers have a built-in capacity.to convert from the language of the user into binary and back again. Most users will not be aware that any conversion is taking place, but it is useful to have the background information for two reasons. First it draws attention to the fact that words can be handled as easily as figures; and, second, it indicates an important area of development in computer technology, to make the conversion technique increasingly sensitive to ordinary written language, and eventually to the spoken word.

The wider issue raised by fears of poor numeracy concerns the skills which are needed to use a computer, and what extra is being required of a social worker. The necessary starting-point to this discussion is to distinguish the generic from the specific definition of 'use'. In its wider form the use of a computer may involve some knowledge of the insides of the equipment as well as techniques for giving the computer a sequence of instructions. This latter is programming. Before a computer can be used to record, recall, alter or in any way process information, it has to be programmed. That is to say it has to be told, logically and in a language it can understand, how to receive the information and what to do with it. There are several programming 'languages' in common use, most of which are recognisably English (or American). Perhaps the best-known is BASIC (Beginners All-purpose Symbolic Instruction Code).

While the advent of less obscure languages may make programming easier for the layman, nevertheless the task of writing a program and checking it for all possible flaws (de-bugging) remains too specialised and time-consuming for the social worker to tackle. In practice programs are usually bought off the shelf (as software packages) or written on the spot by specialist programmers. Hence the relationship between programmer and social worker becomes important if the program is to do its job properly, and this will be picked up later in the chapter.

The narrower definition of 'user' and the one which applies specifically to social workers involves no more than following a set of instructions about getting the equipment to work, and then employing a program written by someone else to do the required task. The 'keying-in' process to Hampshire's computer, described in Chapter 3, is an example. This book is another, a little different, because it is being written and stored on a micro-computer. The process is to turn on the power to computer and TV screen (sometimes to a printer as well if it is going to be used), slot in a small cartridge containing the program and another blank cartridge to record whatever is written, and then type 'Lrun mdv1__Boot' (which stands for 'load and run a program on a cartridge in microdrive number 1 answering to the name of Boot'). The program is, in this case, a word-processing one called Quill, which has a start-up sequence called Boot. It could easily be used to take a client case-file. These initial instructions are on paper, and all later ones appear on the screen. The only skill needed is to be able to use a keyboard which looks and behaves like a typewriter. The most modern programs will even make that easier by correcting spelling mistakes automatically, and having a special key called 'Help' for anyone who wants a bit of guidance.

It would be wrong to underestimate the importance of the typing skill, especially given the hard work needed to develop from a two-fingered amateur into a professional keyboard operator. Many social workers with computer access react to this by using clerical staff to do the work on the terminal. But it is neither an obscure nor an incomprehensible skill, and it is not the sort to provoke fearfulness.

The conviction that a person has a jinx on them whenever it comes to using something like a computer is not so easy to counter. In one sense it is set up as a self-fulfilling prophesy. In another it has a 'folklore' quality to it, in the same conceptual parameters as sod's law, or the belief that the moment you get into a bath the phone will ring. It is difficult to give it any scientific credence, and the claimant may be saying no more than: 'I have no hands and five left feet when it comes to this kind of activity, so give me a miss.' Leaving aside (but not necessarily dismissing) arguments about personal electricity, or poltergeists or the like, a jinx is more likely to be a reflection of a lack of self-confidence than anything else.

The computer, however, stimulates these kinds of fears that people may have a jinx on them, by its occasional erratic behaviour. Within social services departments it is common to find the local authority computer with a reputation for being error-prone or unreliable. The next chapter will consider the impact of inaccuracy on the usefulness of computers in social work practice. At this point it is worth drawing together the three likely causes of something going wrong. The first is a fault in the machinery itself. Computers have established a deserved reputation for reliability as electronic units, and larger ones are routinely put through a maintenance sequence. However, big systems, with a lot of equipment, linking numerous terminals, have a lot of bits which can go wrong. More importantly the communication links of computer to terminals are usually dependent on fallible British Telecom lines, at the mercy of marauding excavators or low-flying wire-cutters. The second is a flaw in the program. One of the pleasures of a computer buff, coming face to face with a new program, is to try to make it collapse, by exposing some error in its structure. The point has been made earlier that the establishment of a new program has both an initial writing phase and a subsequent de-bugging one. Some de-bugging can be done in advance, but ironing out all the flaws usually only follows extensive operational trials. If errors are tiny and of no consequence, or simply reflect odd quirks which the user gets accustomed to handling, nothing may be done, but it is normal practice to provide refined and corrected 'upgraded' versions of a program throughout its operational life.

A user may often feel responsible if something of this sort goes wrong, and indeed may have made the wrong keyboard entry which led to it. But the user certainly should not accept any blame. If a program cannot cope with a user who makes a mess of carrying out instructions it is a bad program.

In contrast the third area of faults does derive clearly from the user (not you, of course, but some other earlier user!), and is the 'garbage in – garbage out' sequence. While a modern computer may be able to check and correct spelling, or draw attention to clearly inappropriate entries, it cannot tell true from false information. Indeed 'true' and false' are meaningless concepts for the computer, unless it is instructed precisely how to tell the difference; all information is accepted at face value, and handed back to later users on the same basis. While this does not indicate any relevant skills for computer users, it does illuminate some virtues, and focus on the crucial point at which information is entered. At this stage the user needs to be systematic, careful and thoroughly diligent in checking and editing all entries before confirming their passage to a data-file. Later users have little choice but to trust the accuracy of the person who first entered the information.

Social workers and programmers

It is a regular comment from social workers that they have no opportunity to understand computer specialists because they never meet, so a myth grows up that computers are run by a kind of subterranean species who speak an alien tongue and rarely emerge to see what is happening in the real world. If we wish to be precise then it is one group of computer staff who are particularly important, containing those who design and write the programs for the personal social services. It is here that social workers should look for some mutual understanding, and some communication.

The origins of difficulties have already been touched on: computers have become surrounded by the mystique of jargon and abbreviation, social workers have their own capacity to be incomprehensible to outsiders, and there are few people who have the training and experience to span the gulf. It is not quite as bad as two groups each speaking a different language, but commun-ication requires a conscious effort to de-mystify and 'secularise' both the written and spoken word. There are many reasons why specialist languages grow up, but perhaps three are worth considering here. One is to provide a means of handling new notions and new 'things'. This is especially important in the development of new sciences and technologies, and much of difficulty with computerese is that it contains labels of this kind, for new types of equipment, components, systems and processes.

While some developments require additions to language, there are others which are not new at all, or perhaps only new in emphasis. That is to say the label for an established concept or process, or item of equipment, takes on an element of novelty or a nuance of meaning which leads to the specialist usage becoming different from the lay understanding. Social work is riddled with examples. Supervision, relationship, contract, referral, allocation – all are words in common everyday usage which also have a distinctive meaning in social work. Disk is another illustration. Originating from 'discus', a flat round object, it became in 1888, according to *The Shorter Oxford Dictionary*, 'a phonograph or gramophone record'. Ask a computer buff today and the definition will be something like 'a means of storing computer data', probably with some added comments about floppy and hard disks. The problem is not so much the wish to be able to identify items and ideas which have a special meaning in computing or social work. This is a necessary part of developing a subject area. The real trouble comes from opting to use words which are already known and used in everyday language, because the result is to stir up confusion for the outsider.

The third reason for setting up a specialist language which is relevant to this context is to enable shorter and faster communication within the specialist group. Sometimes this consists of initials or shortened versions of straightforward labels – RAM for Random Access Memory, MIS for Management Information System, or NFA for No Fixed Abode. Occasionally it becomes more complex, as shorthand for sophisticated concepts or processes which would otherwise take many sentences to describe and define. Here we have the generic labels – psychopath, EMI (Elderly Mentally Infirm), multi-tasking (where a computer does several jobs simultaneously) – which are confusing to the outsider because of their lack of precision, and open to controversy and variable use among insiders. Given time, the unique and specific abbreviations can be learned, but we have a capacity to pick on the same abbreviaitons to mean wholly different things. The example of IT was mentioned in Chapter 1, and it is not the only one. Social workers can confuse themselves with APO as Assistant Principal Officer or Adult Placement Officer, and the rest of the population by using TA as Transactional Analysis rather than Territorial Army. In computing there is a respectable specialised connotation to POKE.

Is there justification for specialised languages in computing and social work? The answer in part has to be that some new labels are unavoidable, and many abbreviations are extremely useful. On the other hand there is a degree of irresponsibility in the way some terms have been allowed to take on a special meaning while they continue to be used differently by the rest of society. Although on the surface there is perhaps more jargon and use of abbreviation in computing than in social work, the regular snorts of complaint coming from social workers about their computer colleagues do tend to suggest a pot being blacked by a decidely tarnished kettle. There has been a genuine need for new labels in computing to reflect the technological developments, and a substantial attempt has been made to educate wider readers in the meaning of computing terms. Many books and journals on computing include a glossary of terms or a beginner's guide (for example the monthly magazine *Personal Computer World* has a regular feature called 'Newcomers Start Here', which explains both jargon and the basic principles of computing). In contrast social workers have made little effort to clear up their own use of jargon, or try to explain it to others.

There appears to be no way of avoiding the difficult first step in communication between social workers and computer staff, which is to gain an understanding of each other's language. Once through the language barrier however, what will be found? Will it be a discovery of kindred spirits, or a more profound realisation of differences? What are the points of contact and of disparity? Any attempt to answer these questions would be both highly speculative and beg all sorts of supplementary queries. Yet there are some points worth making.

Perhaps the most fundamental distancing characteristic is likely to derive from the tasks of working with computers and working with people. Designing and writing a computer program is a precise activity. A program can become enormously complex, and behave with great flexibility, but it must be structured with exactness and written accurately to the last item of punctuation. Flexibility rests on a platform of precision and predictability. Terms like 'being pragmatic', 'making an intuitive response' or 'reacting to an emergency' have no place in the job of computer programming. Nor can a program function with 'loose ends'. The creative skill of a programmer is being able to conceive of and hold on to a network of steps and paths, all going somewhere definite and all precisely linked to each other. It is a bit like being able to take in a complex road map, with its main roads, bypasses, country lanes, diversions, stopping points, road works and dead ends, to see clearly where each track is going and all the alternative possibilities for getting from one place to another.

Social work is in many ways a total contrast. If programming is an attempt to achieve flexibility through precise structuring, social work is often an attempt to establish some sort of structure and coherence out of the chaotic and unpredictable. Far from needing the kind of mind which can work logically from step to step (though that may be what we all profess to do!), social workers need the mental and emotional agility to cope with wholly unexpected and illogical events. More than that, they then have to put together all these loose ends, unanswered questions, seemingly unrelated events and conflicting attitudes into an assessment, a rational explanation and a plan for treatment.

Here, however, is where the tide turns. In one sense social workers are very different from computer programmers, doing a job in dramatically different circumstances, and needing different skills and temperaments. Yet there are some similarities, and they are quite fundamental ones. The task for the social worker in trying to take hold of the history and dynamics of a client, to get them into some sort of perspective and shape, and relate them to the purpose of social servicing, has parallels with the programmer's need to draw together the diverse strands of raw material in a way which allows a desired range of analysis and conclusion to result.

The crux of this argument is that in their work both programmers and social workers are concerned with forms of flowcharting. In computing, a flow-chart 'is simply a method of assisting the programmer to lay out, in a visual, two-dimensional format, ideas on how to organise a sequence of steps or events necessary to solve a problem by a computer' (Hunt and Shelley, 1979, p. 52). The 'sequence of steps' is rather more than just a series of links in a chain because each one indicates some type of activity. In addition to beginning and end-points there are three 'activities'. One is a request to feed in some information; the second a call to take specific action; and the third is a path-finding choice from alternative routes. In computer programming each of these activities is represented visually by a differently shaped link, and the flow-charting process is part of the planning stage of the overall task.

The similarity to some aspects of social work should be getting clearer, and may become more so by offering an illustration. A published set of guidelines for 'Children at Risk' (Leake, 1984) incorporates a flow-chart as an outline reference guide, and the first three steps are examples of the activities listed above. The first is a request for 'Information/observation about a possible abuse', and this leads to the second step, a path-finding question 'Is child on Register?' The choices are 'Yes' or 'No', and both lead to a request for action, in the former 'Contact key worker' and the latter 'Contact social services, police or NSPCC'. The chart continues to a variety of concluding points (care proceedings, voluntary supervision, prosecution or no further action), but already the full range of different activities has been encountered.

One development of this argument will be pursued in Chapter 7, which will suggest that because there are comparable processes in the tasks of social work and computing, there is potential for using computers within social work practice. The ojective at this stage, however, is the more limited one of demonstrating that there is common ground in the way social workers and programmers approach their work, and the sort of common ground that would promote mutual understanding. A vital issue for the future is whether that in itself will be sufficient to enable social workers to realise the full potential of computing, and communicate their needs to computer staff. It is certainly going to be important to avoid institutionalising the position of social workers in the front line and computer staff in the back room, and instead promote regular dialogue.

This chapter started from the premiss that social workers not only had to know something about the things computers can and cannot do, but also had to be encouraged and enabled to become users. It went on to argue a number of points – that there is a difference between programming a computer and using one; that numeracy is not important; that the necessary skills are more in the field of typing than anything else; that there is a problem of jargon on both sides which needs to be tackled; and that there is a basis for communication between social workers and computer people. Coming to some understanding on these points does not of itself provide the case for becoming a user, but it does clear away some of the impediments. The next stage is to look at other impediments, primarily of an ethical and political kind. Providing the social worker can be persuaded over that hurdle, then the prospect for really getting involved with the new technology will rest firmly on establishing just what the computer has to offer for social work. Will the computer settle down as not much more than a management tool, with some uses in social work, but of the kind that can be easily and conveniently left to clerical staff (a recognisable situation in many area offices at present); or can it become an integrated part of social work practice?

6

The Rights and Wrongs of Computing

This is a complex subject. In the first place the arguments involve computers, but are not wholly about them. Some of the major issues are more correctly seen as about communication networks. Other topics have more diffuse origins, but are conveniently hung on to the peg of computing. Still more are based on the growth of computing as a symptom rather than a cause of social and political developments. The subject is also one which has a history of provoking strongly polarised views, from the enthusiast galloping along with the torrent of technological progress (for example, C. Evans, 1979) to the pessimist who sees in computing all the signs of social decay and destruction (such as George, 1977).

There are several tiers of argument. At the most general level is the view that the computer is one of a number of inventions which we could well do without, and should abandon. This is an opinion which is not frequently encountered solely in relation to computing, but can be found in a wider philosophy along with such as nuclear fusion or industrial activities which cause serious illnesses and pollution. Much more common is the modified view that if computing is to be tolerated it must fit into an acceptable social, ethical and political framework for the functioning of our society.

The contrasting attitudes at this level tend to be less concerned with issues of right and wrong than with pragmatic assessments of what would be possible and impossible if we did not use computers. The argument is likely to suggest that, although there may be some unpleasant aspects to computing (as well as to the other components of Information Technology), the truth is that we can no longer do without it. Already we are dependent on computers to cope with the scale of activity needed to run large industrial societies, or even the size of community which makes up a modern city. The supporter can produce a long list of basic services which would collapse without the storage and processing abilities of computers, allied to telecommunication networks.

A somewhat more specific spectrum of views ranges around calculations and speculations about the impact of computing on our society. One of the early studies of this subject (Rose, 1969) suggested five serious problems which would go hand in hand with the rise of computing. The one which has perhaps become most widely apparent is the move towards dehumanising society, especially with the switch from personal communication to machine-produced circulars with no more than a veneer of individuality. Closely linked would be a tendency towards over-systematising many aspects of life, so reducing our capacity to cope with diversity. There would, Rose argued, be a sort of contamination of society by the structured and rigid systems of computing, so that communities would function and be described in more technological terms. Alongside the social drift would come the new elite, the technologists who knew about and controlled computer systems. Finally this knowledge and access available to the new elite would create great possibilities for strong centralised political control, especially as vast data banks of personal information were built up.

The alternative view might be to accept a good deal of Rose's vision, much of which can now be observed to have happened, but to challenge the assumption that such changes are necessarily for the worse. Computers have after all brought enormous benefits in helping us to do things which were becoming too difficult to handle in any other way (like knowing the size and make-up of our communities), and more creatively have enabled a scrutiny of our lives which has uncovered vitally important knowledge (such as the relationship between smoking and cancer). With these kinds of benefits, who should quibble over a few disadvantages?

The sort of person who might have a dusty answer to that question could well be unemployed. In the early years of computer developments a direct and simplistic relationship was asserted between computing and job levels. If a computer could do a task (usually a clerical one) more quickly, effectively and cheaply than people, the computer would be used and the people would lose their jobs. With the benefit of experience the picture which emerges is more complex. Where jobs have been lost to computers in clerical settings, new ones, albeit fewer, have been created to handle word-processors and other new equipment. Computers have, however, spread well beyond clerical employment scenes, and their use to control robots (in car production, for example) suggests a more conscious attempt to displace the labour force. Fry acknowledges the probability of 'significant numbers of former machine operators becoming redundant' (Fry, 1978, p. 176).

This stark and damaging relationship would perhaps have retained its place as one of the major issues of the second half of the twentieth century except for two factors. One has been the world recession, which has resulted in so much unemployment that it has ceased to be possible to pinpoint that which is directly caused by computer applications. This is noticeable in social services departments where general austerity measures have led to a variety of posts being scrapped or frozen, and concealed the specific impact of computerisation. It is also a relevant observation that our personal service agencies have not yet ventured far into computing, and so have still to face the pressure on jobs from that source. The second factor is an agonising ambivalence provoked by the knowledge that job losses are countered by major gains in productivity, which offers scope for a more attractive life-style for all of us. For the moment, however, the policies and methods for a fairer distribution of the spoils of computer exploitation have not been worked out, and the more attractive life-style remains a fantasy for society as a whole.

A further tier of debate draws the computer into the context of specific applications. Accepting the existence and utility of the new technology, is it possible and sensible to clarify those sectors in which its use is desirable and those where it is not? Essentially the issue here is concerned with using the computer in ways which invade individual privacy and threaten civil irghts, even indirectly. Within this argument there are a number of sectors in which the computer is an acknowledged asset – in controlling equipment, helping to plan production lines, working out salaries and many others – but there are also 'no go' areas. Controversy surrounds any computer activity which involves collecting personal information about members of the community, with or without their knowledge and approval. It affects the principle of collecting this sort of data, the way it is stored, the extent to which it is made available to others and the way it is used.

It is at this stage of the debate that social workers' fears are really aroused. The collection of personal information is an integral part of the social work task, and it is social workers themselves who do most of the collecting. Gathering information to help in planning treatment or services has long been an acceptable activity, providing it is suitably hedged around with controls, and carried out in line with professional standards. Getting personal data for the computer is a very different matter, and raises issues which have not as yet been properly thrashed out. A survey of publications on computing in social work concluded that: 'The most recurrent and the most specific concern raised in the literature involved the issue of confidentiality. The general concern was that the very existence of computerised information posed a serious threat to privacy.' (Boyd, Hylton and Price, 1978, p. 370.)

It is not the intention of this chapter to continue skimming over the broad span of arguments, but to set the context and then focus on issues which are likely to be particularly sensitive to social workers. From their viewpoint in the information system social workers can look towards their managers, to the agency and to the wider network of governmental organisations. In this direction they will see issues of accountability, control and centralisation. They can also look outwards towards society, and specifically at their clients, and here they will see the concerns for privacy, confidentiality and respect for individuals. There remains an inner view towards the practices and standards of each worker, which both pinpoints the way traditional activities are handled, like recording and the relationships established with clients, and queries the response made to pressures from new technologies. Each of these perspectives will be looked at in more detail.

Power and the computer

'Information, whether computer processed or not, is an instrument of control, whether of program or, directly or indirectly, of staff.' (Hoshino, 1982, p. 8.) The relationship between the possession of information (or education) and power is as old a theme as is political philosophy itself, and it has always been acknowledged that the more comprehensive the information becomes, the greater the potential for using it as a tool of control. The computer has not, therefore, created a new relationship; instead it has brought an existing one nearer to realisation. Before computers a major impediment to the extension of information systems was their tendency to get so cumbersome as to be of limited use. What the computer has done is to reinforce the capacity to hold vast quantities of data, and added (along with communication techniques) the ability to link together and cross-reference individual items, and to do this, as well as general retrieval, very fast.

The Introduction to this book made the point that computing came into personal social service agencies in the first instance as a management tool, to facilitate a range of useful tasks connected broadly with service planning and accountability to central government and local committees. As the story of Hampshire Social Services Department indicates (Chapter 3) the management team sought an information system which would make policy implementation and resource deployment a more rational process; at the same time more effective (because better informed) arguments could be made to DHSS and the Social Services Committee. A result of this development, possibly not anticipated or intended, has been to increase the accountability of managers to their Civil Service and political masters. By making more information available, managers have opened themselves to more scrutiny from above.

In the early years of social services departments it is doubtful if there was a widespread understanding that what was happening to managers could be extended down the hierarchy. Early information systems were neither thorough nor comprehensive enough to offer much potential, and pressure from tighter control of resources had not yet built up. But by the middle of the 1970s a clearer picture of the scope for controlling social work was emerging. The 1970s were described for social work as 'The Age of Accountability' (Briar, 1973, p. 2), and the point was made that: 'The significance of computer technology to the ordinary agency lies in its potential for integrating the processes of evaluation with delivery of services, thus increasing agency accountability.' (Hoshino and McDonald, 1975, p. 10.)

Any resistance which might have grown among management to

becoming more accountable was mitigated by the undoubted value to them of output from the computer information system. As has already been suggested (and will be again in the next chapter) the value of computers for social workers is far from clearly established, and indeed certain features of the way they have been introduced to computing have not been encouraging. The initial contact for most will have been to provide management information, without, at that stage, any expectation of benefiting themselves. Later, as the information system became more sophisticated, and hence of more potential use to the practitioner, two rather threatening aspects became apparent. One was that the computer could be, and given the economic context was being, used to implement restraints on professional activities with resource implications. An analysis of team workloads, and the range of tasks being carried out, could be used to indicate areas of high and low priority, and allow managers both to direct and monitor social work performance. Closely allied to this, and the second threat, is the ability to use the computer to monitor the performance of individual members of staff.

A manager might well be tempted to ask why 'when computer processed data are used by management for worker performance evaluation, the information constitutes a threat to front-line staff' (Hoshino, 1982, p. 8). After all, it is sound managerial practice to keep this controlling hand on the behaviour of employees. The problem with such a view is that it shows considerable ignorance of the history of social work and the way it is practised. Much social work has grown up as a response to emergencies, or needs which require prompt attention, without scope for prior managerial debate. The traditional basis of social work has been the establishment of the sort of relationship with clients which facilitated intimate discussion, detailed assessment and co-operation over treatment. That is to say a close relationship, and one in which the social worker exercises a lot of discretion. There is a dimension of confidentiality, which will be taken up later, and again a difficulty about relating back to management via a computer or any other information system. These aspects of social work practice have long been recognised, and their retention was supported in the Barclay Report (Barclay, 1982, especially chapter 9), but they do not always seem to find a place in management attitudes, perhaps because they are rarely encountered in a wider sphere of large organisations. It is part of a system in which social workers are too often perceived as no more than skilled employees, while the task they undertake requires much of the autonomy enjoyed by a professional (for further discussion see Glastonbury, Cooper and Hawkins, 1983, chapter 9).

As information systems become more comprehensive and centralised, there is a movement in the location of data which affects convenience of access. With traditional case-files, as with computer files, there will be a range of staff, both practitioners and managers included, who have authorised access. However the physical location of traditional files has made them easy to look at for the immediate group of social workers and supervisors, but less convenient for more senior managers, possibly involving a journey. Without any change in authorisation, the switched location of computer files tips the balance of ease of access more towards the management group, and so offers more incentive or temptation to oversee front-line activity. There is a very thin line between having the knowledge which is appropriate for effective management, and going over the top into material which draws the manager to interfere in the detailed provision of services.

After asserting that 'Control of machinery and its operation is also a political question' Sharron (1984, p. 14) goes on to raise the issue of the cost of computing. Expenditure is incurred both through running costs and capital investment, and represents a diversion of resources away from other activities. As long as computing is kept at a basic level those 'other resources' are likely to be manual information systems, but once into the realm of expensive and sophisticated computer hardware there is a possibility that funds to pay for it will be drawn from service sectors. The question can then be asked about how many social workers, home helps, places in old people's homes or in-service training courses is it worth sacrificing in order to pay for the development of computing? This may be dismissed as a silly question, but it provokes several observations. There is very little indication as yet that agencies have looked beyond the attractiveness and utility of the tasks computers can undertake into a more rigorous cost–benefit analysis, except in the limited context of comparing computing with traditional manual information systems. Social workers with a bent towards collecting social histories are regularly accused of gathering more data than they can ever use;

the same may well be true of the more grandiose computer information stores.

The history of computer developments in social services departments, as adjuncts of management, may well have aided an improvement in managerial productivity. At the same time the 'capitalisation' of management has made more stark the gulf between the support systems available at headquarters and those in front-line offices. The Barclay Committee (Barclay, 1982, paras 9.46–8) drew attention to the poverty of clerical and other supportive aids to practice, and it can be argued that this has lowered both the morale and output of social workers. While, therefore, it may be crude and simplistic to talk about having to choose between spending money on a social worker or a computer, it is wholly relevant to suggest that practice groups may be more in need of investment in support services than their managers. It adds insult to injury for many social workers, a predominantly female group, that in the context of this spending on electronic gadgetry the managerial 'haves' are primarily male, so reinforcing their domination of the personal social services.

Rights and the computer

'With the advent of computers two main points seem to arise. One is the question of what should be private to the individual, which is essentially a political question. The other is . . . security of information . . . which is a largely technical question.' (Brier and Robinson, 1974, p. 277.) The latter has already received comment, and a strong argument can be made to the effect that the agencies have done as much as they can to guarantee that the technical aspects of security have been overcome. We are a long way along the road to eliminating the risk of accidental breaches of confidence, and effective password systems are in operation. The largest remaining area of concern on the technical side of security is to an extent outside agency control. It lies in the links between computers, the 'most vulnerable part of any system' (Ben Knox, *The Times*, 17 July 1984), which will most commonly in this country be British Telecom lines. Using this route to get access to a computer (called 'hacking') is a favourite game of the most knowledgeable computer enthusiasts, though it is more often used to find some usable computer space than extract data (because getting into a computer is a first stage; accessing a file on that computer is a further task). This may be hard to stop, but it can be tracked down, as long as agencies are willing to invest in this kind of detection. A more useful preventive measure is to change aspects of the security system at frequent intervals, and certainly when a member of staff with detailed knowledge of the prevailing system leaves. Knox argues that going to an employee with a grudge against the employer is 'the most common and perhaps most worrying method by which information is obtained' (Knox, *The Times*, 7 August 1984).

The real issue remains, therefore, the political one, as has been made clear in the debate over Data Protection. Does the political will exist to establish boundaries to data banks, and strictly enforced limitations on their uses? Will political decisions be based on expedience and the comparative strength of vested interests, or on a firm assertion of ethical values? Will the resources allocated to enforcing security be sufficient to tackle both the harder criminal aspects, such as computer fraud, and the larger and more shadowy area of illicit access to personal data? An initial reaction to the Data Protection Act 1984 is that it will confirm a lack of political will and secure a victory for vested interests. There have been attempts dating back to 1961 to legislate against the abuse of personal information, but the Act which finally became law in the summer of 1984 is concerned less to inhibit the passage of personal material and more to conform to EEC regulations, thereby lubricating the flow of computer data across member countries. The Act sets boundaries for gathering and using personal data, asserts the principle of everyone having access to his or her own file, and requires all holders of stores of such data to register with a Registrar, appointed by the Home Secretary. Each holder must both keep to the general terms of the Act, and to the specific particulars of data sources and uses which form part of the application to register.

The snail-like pace to legislation is matched by the length of time permitted for the Home Secretary, Registrar and data holders to get themselves organised, and it is likely to be well into 1987 before there is any enforcement of breaches of the Act. Even then they will take the form of raps on the knuckles from the Registrar, rather than decisive action. Yet the real weakness of the

Act, and a gaping hole in personal data protection, lies in the exemptions. There are total exemptions from registration (such as for mailing lists, or files classed as official secrets), exceptions to the right of access to one's own file, and limits to confidentiality. We are denied access to our own files if they are deemed to be serving a purpose connected with law and order (so we cannot find out about such possible contents as false accusations of illegal behaviour), or can broadly be labelled as legally privileged. It is left to the Secretary of State to decide on the principle and conditions of client access to social work files. We may think that the information in those files is confidential (except, that is, to what may be a long list of registered recipients), but it must be disclosed if requested in the interests of national security, law enforcement or revenue purposes, or if ordered by a court.

The position is highly polarised. On one side are ranged the police and other forces of law and order (possibly including the military), whose task in preventive policing and large-scale social control is made much easier if continually up-dated information is available about anyone who might conceivably be a 'risk'. Hanging on to their coat-tails are an assorted collection of businesses involved in advertising, marketing, debt-collecting, vetting credit-worthiness and so forth, who are prepared to pay large sums and sometimes get into illicit activities in order to lay hands on computer data. Support is also likely from governmental bodies wanting to check for tax dodgers, false benefit claims, unreported house alterations which might breach planning regulations or alter rateable values, CND activists ... the list is endless.

At the other pole is a grouping of those with a concern or responsibility for civil rights, and a range of professionals whose work has traditionally required them to be on the receiving end of personal information. The fear for many of these people is that the deluge of technological innovation has exposed information sources to exploitation before the risk was fully realised and closed off. This in turn has allowed traditional attitudes towards the confidentiality of personal data to be pushed aside and replaced by newer precedents which set much wider and freer access. In short, professionals and civil rights activists were caught on the hop, hustled out of step by the pace of growth in computing and communicating.

The issue in civil rights is the continuing one of protecting the individual against the invasion of government and organisations. To that extent the threat posed by computers represents nothing new, except in its scope and dynamics. Similar fears about the effects of gathering information in standardised forms have been expressed about many systems of organisation and administration, especially bureaucracy. As Harrington states: 'Bureaucracy is the only way to co-ordinate the complex functions of a modern economy and society. ... Yet it is also an enormous potential source of arbitrary, impersonal power which folds, bends, spindles and mutilates individuals but keeps IBM cards immaculate' (quoted in George, 1977, preface). The mere enlargement of organisations is itself a threat to privacy, and the merger of small welfare agencies into social services departments had the effect of increasing the number of those with authorised access to any individual file.

George (1977, chapter 3) has enlarged on the concept of 'information pollution' as a way of analysing the abuse of personal data, and drawing attention to the distorting sequences through which information is put from the point of its initial gathering through to its application for some organisational purpose. The data themselves may contain inaccuracy, which is then embedded so firmly in data stores as to be irremovable. The numerous steps in data handling, the tendency to twist it until it can be fitted into one of a restricted range of categories and the attempt to use it in quite different ways from that in which it was collected – all serve to pollute the quality of the material. The pollution is then spread around by all those firms and government agencies who make use of the files.

In his assessment of the trends in information abuse, George suggests a number of stages, starting with the spreading around of fairly trivial data, like people's addresses, which we have now grown to accept. The next stage reflects both the growing comprehensiveness of the data, and thoroughness of its distribution, all of which indicates a clear invasion of individual privacy. The final stage sees the gap closed between intrusiveness and interference, so that computerised information becomes the basis for ordering individual lives. Despite the belated efforts to provide some sort of data protection legislation (which could still become as much a charter for exploitation as for protection) the evidence appears to suggest that we are already well into the middle stage, and beginning to edge towards the final one. There is considerable circumstantial support for the view that much information collected through statutory processes (such as Censuses) or given by the individual in confidence (for example, in a request for a bank loan) finds its way to organisations who wish to use it for business purposes. The Registrar-General has sold Census material. At the time of writing (summer 1984) a major bank is being accused in the media of leaking private financial information, and the Consumers' Association (May and July 1984) is concerned that a credit card company is getting personal transactions muddled.

In most circumstances the person who offers information 'in confidence' will have a wholly unreal picture of what happens to it, who has legitimate access, where it will be passed or the uses to which it will be put. Despite some limited individual rights, most of us are equally vague about what is in the file. Indeed many people may not have provided information at all, and a file will only contain data obtained from second-hand sources, with the risks of hearsay and guilt by association.

The issue of confidentiality takes on added nuances for the professional (doctor, social worker), community confidante (priest) or anyone else (bank manager, employer) whose work inevitably calls for gathering personal information. Such people may in the past have been able to see themselves as the sole repositories of the confidence, but the pressure is on them to become (whether from conviction, money, lack of thought, accident, legal requirement or simply by turning a blind eye) the first links in a chain of data collection and management. Focusing specifically on the social worker, the problem is not entirely new. Social workers have always retained discretion under certain circumstances to pass on information about clients, and have not necessarily had client sanction to do this. There are well-established procedures, perhaps most obviously case conferences, where information is offered for discussion and decision to other staff of the agency as well as other agencies. The legitimate possibilities for passing data were touched on in Chapter 3 when looking at Hampshire Social Services Department's rules of conduct for using computer files, and it was suggested that social workers might feel a little more inclined to question this arrangement when it is formally spelled out rather than just allowed to happen. The exercise of discretion seems to be more open to individual professional judgement than a written statement of policy, and so more acceptable to the worker.

A problem which has been exacerbated by the new technology is that once an information chain is started it is very difficult to bring it to an end or change it, and those who forged the first links rapidly lose any control over the process. Information is like money – once you hand it to someone else it is no longer yours, and all you can be reasonably sure about is that a little bit of it may be saved, but most will be passed on and eventually go into general circulation.

There is certainly a difference in scale – only data on selected individuals will be handed out at a case conference, in contrast to the massive blocks of material in the dealings discussed earlier – but legitimate practices are far from leak-proof. Part of the difficulty lies in the absence of a generally accepted code of conduct, so that although a social worker may be scrupulously careful about giving information away, the recipients could be operating a quite different code, and feel rather freer about using information in their hands.

Social work standards and the computer

A review of published comments about the threat the computer poses to standards of social work performance unearths a number of sturdy views. Professor Tutt is reported (*Community Care*, 10 February 1983, p. 6) to have argued that 'The sacred cow of confidentiality and privacy is not a defence for old ways of working', and pressed social workers to take a more positive and creative view of computing. A more frequently stated view, however, upholds a greater respect for traditional practices: 'Unless clients and social workers alike can be guaranteed adequate measures to ensure a similar level of privacy as previously existed, the client-worker relationship may be under-mined.' (Powell, 1980, p. 17.) Sharron takes the argument a stage further, suggesting that 'practice will also tend to become more standardised and social work by strict objectives will inevitably, for better or worse, become the order of the day' (1984, p. 14).

Many aspects of this debate have already received an airing – the threat that the computer will increase breaches of confidentiality from a dribble to a deluge, and that control of information could be used to inhibit the flexibility of practice – but the question remains as to whether standards of practice will be put at risk. The recurring themes are confidentiality, the client–worker relationship and professional discretion, and it may be helpful to summarise the attitudes of those who are fearful of the computer's future role.

As for confidentiality, it is not total at present, but leaks are small and containable: the computer will take the personal social services into an entirely different league, with huge transfers of private data, by accident, illicit behaviour or conscious decision. If the social worker is to be part of a network of data-gathering, a contributor to data banks, then it will no longer be possible to talk intimately and privately to clients. The relationship will therefore be affected, and will become more formal and guarded. It will be harder to provide good assessments, and the trusting and co-operative relationship which is at the root of effective counselling will be wiped out. The utility of the relationship will be further reduced by the ability of a computer-informed management to interfere in traditional areas of discretion, so damaging the credibility of the pactitioner and adding rigidity to the process.

The core of this viewpoint is recording. If data are not recorded, or are held on files which are inaccessible to all but the social worker, the threat to social work practice is removed. Without records, whether they are loose-leaf files or a computer store, there would be little risk of either large- or small-scale abuse of information. Why are records so vulnerable? One reason is that social workers have already lost a sense of clarity about the use of them, and have permitted them to serve so many diverse purposes. A selection might include:

- reminding the social worker of the progress of a case
- recording services and resources offered
- offering notes for professional supervision
- providing evidence for reviewing worker performance
- giving a basis for looking at overall workloads
- acting as a handover document for a new worker
- covering the staff in the event of an inquiry.

This list is not comprehensive, and includes only uses made by the worker, the immediate team and the professional supervisor. Still more precedents include using traditional files for management and research purposes, broadly along the same lines as a computer file might be used. Further trends may well involve opening records to clients, and that event would be more effective than computerisation in forcing a reappraisal of the content and use of files.

The point being made is that for decades records have served multiple purposes, going far beyond what would be sanctioned solely on grounds of relevance to the client–worker relationship and the social work task. Indeed anyone who has looked at a sample of traditional files is quite likely to have found a shambles, a wad of papers without apparent structure, order or purpose. The computer should not be used as a scapegoat for the mess we have got into over case files.

It is possible to pass an equally sceptical eye over some aspects of the client–worker relationship, which has been put under great pressure by increasing agency workloads, and the temptation to use time-saving methods of social work intervention. The relationship is an aspect of traditional forms of practice which presupposed sufficient time in each interview and in the duration of the client–worker contact to allow intimacy to develop. With some of the more time-limited approaches the social worker may still pay lip-service to a relationship, but it runs the risk of being artifical and forced. Given the proportion of very brief contacts in many area offices, especially with intake work, it is scarcely possible to pretend at a relationship. Instant social work like instant coffee is definitely not the real thing, and it is appropriate to ask precisely what computing is supposed to be putting under threat.

Fears that computer information systems might be used by managers to facilitate easier interference in front-line activities are perhaps more firmly based. Many managers are themselves ex-practitioners, liable to maudling nostalgia about the good old days of working with clients (and forgetting the bad pay and long hours!). The temptation is there to use any means of keeping in touch with the trenches from the safety of a managerial armchair. More importantly there are sound management arguments for using whatever tools are available to ensure that the agency works properly to policy and plan. The existence of social worker discretion to act within flexible boundaries rather than to precise regulations is a source of much frustration for the manager who is wanting to keep a tight hold on the way the agency functions. The fat volumes of procedural guidelines for social workers are a visible sign.

These last few paragraphs have been intentionally provocative, in order to make clear the risk of hiding behind the computer and blaming it for weaknesses which have their origins elsewhere, whether in the behaviour of social workers or their managers. Furthermore, a distinction needs to be made between the impact of decisions about the way the personal social services will function in the future, and changes which will be caused by computers. It is very likely that knowledge about the sorts of tasks the computer can aid will influence the decisions which are made, but the computer is the tool not the handyman. The decisions will be made in the context of politics and administration, both of which social workers can influence if they get their act together. Computers can do a lot of jobs, some helpful, others a hindrance to social workers. Control of the computer is vital.

Some proposals

This chapter has not attempted to offer a balanced view of the politics of computing. The case for the computer – primarily the near impossibility of doing without it – has been stated, but much more attention has been paid to the other side of the argument, the fears and reservations expressed about where the new technology is leading us. The reason for this is embedded in the sound social work principle of taking account of initial preoccupations, in order to make space for a more reflective approach. It is clear that before the full potential of the computer can be realised, in a form which is helpful to social work practice, an acceptable context has to be set to take account of genuine fears and reservations.

Several efforts have been made, both in the setting of computing and in social work. Brier and Robinson (1974, p. 279) suggest five stages to a code for data processing, primarily drawn from the ethics of social science research. Their sequence starts by asserting initial confidentiality, which is then reinforced by checking all data to remove identity marks, such as names and addresses, and replacing them with coded alternatives. Points 3 and 4 state who shall have the necessary information to interpret the codes (in research only the researcher), and stress the importance of formally considering all aspects of individual protection before publishing. The final point draws attention to the further need for individual protection if raw data are to be made available to another researcher.

Within social work NALGO is prepared to wait and see, noting some of the advantages of new technology, but also expressing some concerns and concluding that 'experience is varied' (NALGO, 1984, p. 52). The British Association of Social Workers has produced a sequence of project group reports and policy statements (1972, 1975, 1980, 1983) related to proper conduct and standards in social work, which do not tackle computing head-on, but offer a sound framework for so doing. In particular the project group report on 'Effective and Ethical Recording' lists 96 recommendations (pp. 46–55) which seek to sort out the muddle of record systems as well as spell out the ethical and practical requirements in collecting, storing, accessing and using personal data.

Trying to draw together aspects both of social work and computing, as discussed in this chapter, a number of proposals can be suggested as a contribution to getting computers fully and properly used in social work:

1. The establishment of a legal framework covering bulk data distribution and use should be based solidly on a recognition of civil rights, rather than on the practices and precedents of particular segments of society. At present it appears that the law will be much too influenced by vested interests, particularly those of the police and other forces of law and order. However, much of the debate on data protection has tended to consist of small groups claiming special priviledges for themselves, whether it is the police wanting access to everything, or doctors, priests and social workers wanting unique protection. The difficulty in this kind of discussion is that, in their own context, everyone is right. A more effective approach may be to look upon personal information less as something which must automatically be shared with a policeman or treated as a social worker's secret, and more as the

possession of the individual who is the subject of it.

2. Whatever laws are passed, they are likely to need filling out with a code of conduct, both to guide those with access to data, and to save the whole subject becoming enmeshed in legal action and precedent. Such a code needs to extend well beyond social work, certainly far enough to include the network of direct contacts with other agencies, and the more peripheral links in information chains. Some form of Data Protection Panel would be needed to enforce the code and deal with misconduct, possibly with a right of appeal to such a panel from individual subjects of information (such as social work clients have in Holland).

3. In order to cope with the tendency for chains of data to be formed, it is important to have both clear statements of the circumstances in which data may cross an agency boundary (such as Hampshire has), and contracts with potential recipient agencies defining the limits on their use of material passed to them.

4. Some controls should be established over the format and procedures for data transfers from one computer source to another. This is to avoid the temptation to do what comes conveniently, which is to open a computer link from one source to another, rather than transfer a specified item of data as a single transaction. An open computer link is almost certain to result in more data, probably about different people, being transferred than was intended.

5. Consideration should be given to the whole interrelationship between computers and communication networks. Too often it is taken for granted that computer networks are more desirable than self-contained computers. The point is that a self-contained computer is much less open to abuse because it cannot be accessed from another computer via the network line. There needs to be some way of assessing the case for joining a network, based on an estimate of uses and risks. Tighter procedures could also be introduced for turning off the network link except when it is in authorised use, instead of leaving an open connection.

6. The location of personal information in a social work agency has always been in the social workers' office. The implication of developing a comprehensive computer system is that data will be relocated at agency headquarters instead of or in addition to the front-line siting. The need for this should be carefully assessed. The requirements of management are for anonymous aggregate

data, broken down by team, perhaps by worker, but not by named client. In the early years of computing the best way to do this was to use the centralised computer, which inevitably led to the data store being at headquarters. The state of technology now makes it feasible for data stores to be held in the traditional location, at the front-line, which is the only place where there is a justified access to the full details of individual files. This proposal, which is a fundamental one, is that computer case-files should be held only in front-line offices, under the professional control of the social workers whose clients are on those files. Aggregate data should be provided to headquarters for statistical, monitoring and planning purposes. The only centralised file should be of names and the office of case-file location, to permit new referrals to be checked for previous contacts and services. The effect of this proposal would be to return responsibility for client information to the social worker and the immediate team. The proposal does not apply to resource files, such as information about residential and day-care settings, which seems likely to continue to need central- ised handling.

Most of the above proposals are of a general nature, but the last one is central to social work, and without its implementation the future for the computer in practice settings is limited. Either social workers will keep it at as great a distance as possible, because it is out of their control, or they will give it resigned acceptance as the holder of the 'formal' information system, while maintaining an 'informal' system for genuine use.

7

Computers and the Daily Life of Social Workers

This chapter follows a similar line to the previous one, in that it continues to give an airing to the reservations social workers may have about allowing computers into their work. Several of the same themes will surface, but instead of looking at them from a political or ethical viewpoint, the focus will move to the way they impinge on the day-to-day tasks of the social worker. The broad aim of the chapter is to discuss the background and seek a response to two questions a social worker might feel inclined to pose: 'What effect will the computer have on my job?' and 'What's in it for me?' It is probably most helpful to think of these questions as shrouded in overtones of suspiciousness and a little cynicism, because they do reflect fears about what will happen to direct work with clients, about the extra chores that will emerge and about what might be called the 'interfering computer'.

Throughout the chapter some views expressed by social workers will be stated, and these are drawn from informal discussions with practising front-line workers who, on a ratio of about two to one, are involved with a computerised information system. On one point they were all agreed – the forward march of computing is inevitable, and no Canutish actions will stop it. The task, therefore, is not to oppose it, but to accommodate and harness it as effectively as possible. Even so, the topic remains an unreal one unless certain premises are accepted. There will need to be solutions to the political issues discussed in the last chapter. In the absence of satisfactory arrangements about, for example, data protection, social work is either likely to go through a period of discontent and disarray, or be forced to change into something rather different, probably towards an explicit social policing role.

The discussion to follow assumes that social work will keep most of the characteristics it currently has, and in particular that it will continue as a helping profession based on the consent of clients rather than compulsion, on scope for flexible responses at the front-line and on the guarantee of confidential client–worker relationships.

The other range of assumptions are of a more mundane, practical kind, though perhaps less certain of becoming reality in the near future. They concern the availability of the physical resources for social workers to draw upon. It will be of no use discussing the impact of computers on practice, or (as Chapter 8 does) postulating the diverse jobs the computer could do, if the equipment is not there in front of the social workers. It is important to be clear about this. At present most social workers will either have no direct contact with computers in their work, or will be able to use a terminal, possibly a micro-computer, which is shared with several other staff. The limit of ambition for many social services departments is a terminal or two in each area office, where, if current experience is anything to go by, most 'hands on' jobs will be done by a member of the clerical staff. This will certainly achieve some useful outcomes, but it is not the level of equipping which will be needed for practice uses. For any real extension of computing into social work a keyboard and screen (probably also some localised storage capacity like a disk drive) will need to be as accessible as a telephone, and each team will want a printer. In effect this means either a terminal or a micro-computer for each social worker; otherwise the advantage of convenience will ensure the survival of traditional ways of doing the job, with the computer slotting in occasionally if it happens to be free. Social workers cannot do their chores properly if they have to spend time in a queue for access to a terminal or wait for a clear screen before they can check a point in a client's file. The arguments presented earlier about the advantages to managers of going on-line and having immediate computer access, are even more important in front-line activity, with its component of emergencies, clients in the waiting-room and demands for instant information, advice and aid. In short, if computers are to move into social work practice, there have got to be enough of them around, and that means many more than we have or plan to have at present.

The attitude of management in the personal social services will be crucial to the future of computing in social work practice. While many social services departments have been able to launch into computing on the cheap, by tailoring a limited system to take advantage of spare computer capacity in the local authority, developments are expensive. The more sophisticated the system becomes, even if it remains primarily for managerial uses, the greater is the need to purchase computer terminals and other peripherals, perhaps to get computers as well. A push into social work practice would have major resource implications. Social workers have traditionally received little captial investment to support their activities, and it will need strong and effective arguments from managements to their committees to get backing for a change. It is highly unlikely that any arguments will lead to the necessary spending unless there are tangible expectations for greater front-line productivity.

A further sign of managerial good faith will be needed to reverse the trend of information control, as was discussed in the last chapter, to re-establish professional responsibility for case-files. A worrying aspect of the extent to which data-management processes have already been used to alter practice is the way some essentially social work tasks have changed purpose. An illustration is the reception of clients by an intake team or a duty social worker. Traditionally and professionally this is part of the task of assessing client needs and beginning to establish a relationship. More recently reception of new clients has been as much concerned with straightforward data collection. Indeed a computer journal has described the purpose of the referral system in Hillingdon as 'to provide senior management with details of what kinds of people visited the department for social work help, the kinds of problems they faced and, in broad terms, what kind of help they had been given' (Hayman, 1980, p. 87).

All social work processes which involve collecting information of the kind needed in the agency data bank are at risk of being put under pressure to change to suit the convenience of central storage. The minimum change is to set up a standardised format for the data, so that it can fit the structure of the computer program. To be more precise the computer will (as programmed for a management information system) receive material in a prearranged sequence, and each individual item will have to be stated or categorised in a specific way. One way to do this is for the social worker to conduct a conventional interview, say a reception interview, as part of the process of assessment, and then extract from that the information wanted for the computer. The trouble with this approach is that the computing becomes an extra chore, so the temptation, both for busy social workers and their managers, is to try doubling up. The data format for the computer then features in the interview, becomes a determinant of the way the interview is conducted, and can serve as a kind of questionnaire to be filled in. At some point the whole process swings from a social work interview to a data collection interview, and this implies differences in content, sequence and interviewing technique. A detailed US study of just this aspect concludes that 'The largest single obstacle to implementation of the [computer] system was finding a way to collect data about case activity.' (Phillips, Dimsdale and Taft, 1982, p. 135.) Unfortunately the authors see the issue primarily from the viewpoint of the managers and computer staff, presenting the social workers as having no justifiable grounds for their resistance, other than that a new system would expose their traditional inefficiency.

The important factor to pursue is that the computer provides temptation and pressure to change social work practices, coming both from managers and the practitioners themselves, and often aimed at greater convenience and speed. Some aspects of the change may be welcome, as ways of tackling known weaknesses in practice. Included here might be the move towards a more structured approach to recording, and the improvement of casefiles. Other pressures may be unwelcome but transitory, to do with the particular problems of getting a computer system under way – de-bugging the programs, coping with backlogs, commissioning the equipment, finding staff and other resources to cope with the new tasks, and generally handling teething difficulties. Perhaps the biggest problem here has stemmed from coping with the inaccuracies emerging from starter systems (though it is something of an act of faith to equate inaccuracy with teething troubles and no more!) More worrying are what LaMendola calls 'the occurrence of unintended or unanticipated consequences' (LaMendola, 1982, p. 52). He advocates a thorough planning phase to minimise risks of this sort, but acknowledges that there will still be a place for surprises. Some may be helpful, like that clients may find computers easier to 'talk to' than real people, other less desirable, like social workers abandoning interactions with colleagues in favour of communing with the terminal. Two unwanted consequences (from a social work viewpoint) have, however, been widely anticipated, and these will now be considered.

The dehumanising computer

The argument has already been rehearsed. In essence it is that the computer is a machine; substitute a machine for a social worker or put one between the worker and client and the system becomes impersonal and automated. The client ceases to receive a personal service, and the client's circumstances are no longer treated as unique and special. The social worker becomes no more than a service dispenser, and the client–worker relationship, which is the bed-rock of counselling, is lost.

Three comments have been made in earlier chapters on this subject. First, the issue is not solely concerned with the nature of the computer as a piece of equipment, but with the way it is used. As machines go, the computer is extraordinarily flexible. Second, the computer will not replace the social worker, or force its way between worker and client, unless a political decision is made to that effect. The relationship of computer to social worker is not like, say, that of car to horse and cart, a more modern device taking over from an obsolete one. By the time computers can be designed to replace the social worker virtually all work in society will have been taken over by them, and that is the stuff of science fiction. Third, social workers have already compromised on issues of principle and modified their behaviour to suit current work pressures, and nothing is achieved by blaming the computer unfairly. In particular the idea of social work being about a gradually developing relationship with a client, involving a single social worker, has been badly damaged by creations such as intake teams, long-term teams, short-term teams, any arrangements which chop up the overall contact with a client into a series of segments.

What does or can the computer do to dehumanise social work?

It may be helpful to consider this question in four different scenarios:

- – the computer in the background, for information
- – the computer on the social worker's desk, as an aid
- – the computer for clients to handle
- – the computer as bearer of instructions.

The minimal use of the computer, as a background source of information for the social worker, drawing on a management information system, reflects the realistic position of many front-line staff. The most frequent uses are for client and resource checks, and a majority of social workers appear to welcome this facility. The computer is not likely to be on the social worker's desk, or in any spot where it would be visible during a meeting with a client, so it does not intrude physically. Nevertheless by confining a computer to a management information system there is a risk that it will inhibit the flexibility of social work processes in the way mentioned earlier; that is by tempting or pushing the practitioner into organising client contacts to fit the format of the data system. The risk is present both in providing and drawing on data. In the former the social worker will soon grow familiar with the items of material requested for the computer, and may get into the habit of collecting them from the client regardless of the appropriateness of the circumstances. Perhaps a more concealed risk is on the other side of the coin, of getting out of the habit of collecting some information, however useful it might be, if it is not needed for the computer. The social worker is therefore tempted to fall into the trap of standardisation, and where time has to be given to providing data for the computer it can be at the price of failing to keep traditional files as detailed and topical as would be helpful. In short the social worker can get bad habits from the computer, and become slack about the alternative form of recording.

Using computer data can have a similar impact. Just as information is entered in a standardised form and sequence, so it is presented back. If it becomes more convenient to call up a computer display than to fetch and search a folder, the social worker can get to accept and work within the limitations of the computer file. Two points are relevant here. Computer files do not have to be limited to outline information: they can be designed to hold comprehensive material, but in the context of a management information system such detail is not needed, and simply clutters the computer. Further, client data does not have to be standardised unless it is wholly or partly to be used for aggregate analysis – statistical tables, for example. While this is an important managerial function, it is not much wanted by social workers, who on most occasions will want data about specific individuals.

The minimum system, in which social workers are peripheral users of a management information system, is more likely to dehumanise practice than having a more substantial involvement with computers. The reason is that the more social workers use computers, the more programs will be made available with their needs in mind. This is already well illustrated in the small number of applications for offering direct help to the treatment process. For example, the Community Information Project, while stressing the practical difficulties of getting the program to work with the desired level of sophistication, suggests that 'computers are ideally suited to providing personalised advice about welfare benefits entitlement' (Community Information Project, *Computanews*, 1984). Note the assertion that the computer can do a personalised job, in circumstances where a social worker may only be competent to make general comments, albeit with personal charm. The distinction is between the medium and the message – a personal message from the impersonal medium that is the computer, or the reverse from the social worker. If the computer is allowed to be around while the 'relationship' is happening, and be used as a social worker's aid, then both medium and message can be personal.

The variety of experiments to get a good welfare rights system cross the boundary between the computer as an aid and the computer as a tool to be used directly by the client. Some schemes have tended to take the view that an intermediary is necessary, whether a specialist or someone such as a social worker, who will have enough experience of the system to know how to feed in the required data correctly (the essence of a welfare rights programme is that a great deal of material has to be provided to the computer before any answers can be given). The client responds to a human face, and is protected from the technological deterrent of having to work the equipment. This is seen both as more 'user-friendly' and a means of making the task easier for the claimant. On the other hand the DHSS trial (see Chapter 4) offered claimants direct access to a keyboard, and in that way a semblance of privacy was maintained while personal financial information was keyed in. This direct use of the computer can still be linked with social work contact, partly to help those who find it difficult to do the job themselves, and partly to discuss and counsel how the client can respond to the computer output.

The development of both of these kinds of approach, possibly as alternatives from which the client can choose, does not in any substantial way dehumanise the client–worker relationship, or the wider client–agency service contact. In some circumstances the computer will aid the effectiveness of the service being offered to the client, contributing both to the quality of the relationship and the client's satisfaction.

A genuine fear for some social workers is contained in the final scenario, in which the computer becomes the instantly available communication link between front-line worker and HQ manager. Furthermore the fear is that if the equipment is installed, for whatever creative and helpful purpose, control will be its ultimate use. The scene is one which has the social worker feeding data into the central bank instantly, as they are gathered, with a manager or a programmed computer at the receiving end sending back instructions as to what action should be taken next. The social worker becomes not much more than an intermediary between the electronically equipped manager and the client, except for the purposes of taking whatever unpleasantness the client may feel about the interaction. It is certainly the stuff of nightmares, especially if the imagination leads a little further along the line of technological development to the point where the computer terminal is also a microphone transmitting a client–worker interview straight back to the centre.

Although there has to be more dependence on conviction than evidence, it is highly unlikely that such a situation could ever come about. To start with it has to be put in its technological context, for by the time the knowledge and equipment are available for that kind of activity, we shall be in a different world. Many of life's activities will be computerised, clients may use a terminal to contact their social worker and the face-to-face aspect of many jobs may have vanished. There will not be a unique and isolated technological path leading solely to tormented social workers! More realistically, at least for the foreseeable future, the cost would be prohibitive, and it requires an extraordinary amount of cynicism to believe that political approval would be given.

Returning to the question – will the computer dehumanise social work? – the answer is that much depends on the attitudes of social workers. Keep the computer at arm's length and the task of feeding into the management information system may be dehumanising for worker and client. Create increasing demands for specific practice uses and the computer offers the potential for improving the quality of the service and even, at times, making it more personal.

Extra work, productivity and the computer

One social worker described the current uses of computers in the personal social services as 'wasting everyone's time'. It is certainly a prevalent view that the computer does represent extra work for the social worker, with health risks (Whaley, 1983, p. 16) and inadequate returns. How real is the assertion that there is more work involved? If so, what does the computer offer by way of greater productivity?

The suggestion has already been made that there are two major areas of extra work. One is transitory, and is the process of setting up a computer system, taking in the backlog of data, trying to get them accurate and de-bugging the programs. 'Transitory' is an elastic concept, which in a complex system may mean as much as five years. But the other more fundamental cause lies in the creation of dual information systems, one computerised, one manual. The base-line for all social work agencies is a manual system, in which the enormous bulk of material is contained in individual client files. Each of these is likely to contain factual items, a history of events, a record of contacts with the agency staff and use of agency resources and a range of analytical comments, from full assessments and reviews to occasional remarks on a scrap of paper. Drawn from these files will be summarising material, usually in the form of a card index containing some basic facts, which in turn are the source of statistical compilations.

In practice the starting-point for computer systems in the personal social services has been the card index, and not the bulk of raw material in case-files. The reasons are clear enough – the card index was small enough to be manageable, contained the right sort of data (facts) and offered all that was needed for statistical returns. There is no tradition of managers being interested in the minutiae of case-files, unless there is a tragedy or a scandal. Furthermore the early management systems wanted enough accuracy for composite statistics, which meant that occasional errors were not a problem (a 'swings and roundabouts' self-correction was assumed). Precision in each individual file was not a high priority target, and indeed only becomes vital as social worker uses increase.

The combined picture, therefore, is of two systems with different base-lines, structures, contents, uses and objectives, and it becomes very easy to conclude that an agency needs both. If this view is accepted – as it has been almost universally, at least for the present – the upstart computer system shows up clearly as an additional dimension to the workload. In so far as social workers have to provide information for the computer, it makes an extra job for them. To the extent that the same information is held on both manual and computer files there is duplication, but that is the price of having tailor-made systems both for managers and practitioners.

This is the simplistic part of the analysis, from which the 'extra work' assertion arises. Yet there are more complex and devious paths. It is clear that social workers who have been involved for some time with the dual system have begun to compensate for the additional work by making use of the computer system for their own purposes. In part this is the process of getting the computer to do things which are helpful to the social work task, like checking for what is known of a new referral or calculating a client's Social Security entitlements. In this way the additional work leads to a better quality of outcome and possible also a greater quantitative productivity.

There is also compensation for social workers in that they can use their own power point in the computer system to influence the actions of managers. This is a theme developed in detail by Dery in his study of welfare agencies in California (1981). The scene Dery describes is on a larger scale, but has some parallels with a social services department, and the computer story is about efforts to set up a statewide information system, to monitor, co-ordinate and control activities in the smaller areas, the counties. He found that 'Almost anything recorded by the computer is controlled manually by workers. Workers keep track of caseloads, changes in eligibility status, renewal dates, and so does the computer. Though a central feature of the system is the automatic grant computation, workers compute the grants manually. Workers keep manual controls as if the computer did not exist. . . .' (pp. 175–6).

In California the computer system was not trusted or used by workers because it was inaccurate: the workers knew it was inaccurate because they had made it so. Once it is realised that social workers do not have to depend on computer information, but can continue to keep their own, and that managerial uses will include determining staffing and resource levels according to what they are told about workloads, it becomes a temptation to feed the system with the messages field staff would like managers to have. This is not difficult because managers are wholly dependent on social workers for the raw material of agency activities. Clients can be categorised as having needs which put them into a high priority group, when in reality they are not; cases can be kept open on the computer files when they have been closed; or casual inquiries can be recorded as genuine referrals. Dery quotes a Californian manager as allowing for 'fudge', and saying: 'They always come with high figures knowing that I'll cut around 10%' (p. 177).

There is no evidence that British social workers have yet started to behave in a similar way, but it may be sensible to keep such prospects in mind if dual data systems are to become a long-term feature. The message is that social workers can gain some recompense for the extra work, perhaps even welcome it, because of the influence it gives them. By a careful selection of entries to the computer system a favourable image can be presented of the nature and vlume of work undertaken; and by the tactical exclusion of some material a degree of confidentiality can be ensured. This becomes the 'only way in which they [the social workers] retain channels of evocation which they could control on their own terms' (Dery, p. 210). Furthermore, once it comes to be recognised that built-in inaccuracy is endemic to computer information systems, then a political point is made, because the errors which would make it unusable as a source of data for social work practice also makes it unreliable as personal information for any other users, whether inside or outside the agency.

The picture is not a very happy one. A dual system is costly on resources and staff time, and runs the risk of institutionalising distorted social worker–management communications. The alternative is a return to a single system, either by abandoning computing (probably unthinkable) or by moving to a totally computerised arrangement. Some aspects of a unitary approach have already been mentioned – the implication for capital expenditure of equipping social work offices, the need to change the structure of the programs to make them more suitable for individualised material, and the political dimension of data control and confidentiality. The history of computing in our personal social services has given systems the characteristics appropriate to their initial aims and uses, which is standardisation geared to producing composite analysis. If a social services department is to establish a computer system to replace rather than superimpose itself on the manual arrangements, it will need to be based firmly on the characteristics of social work recording schemes. That is to say, each computer client file will need to contain much the same material as do the traditional case-files and card indexes. Most of it will therefore be unique, non-standardised social history, assessment, review, contacts and so forth, and a small part will be factual material suited to composite working.

Moving in this direction has many more implications. The storage capacity of the agency's computing resources will need to be increased substantially, though bearing in mind the political arguments this would involve a number of separate small computers rather than a single large centralised one. The programs would need to be redesigned away from their statistical origins (one of the very earliest client information systems used SPSS – Statistical Package for the Social Sciences) towards a much more fluid and flexible form of storage and display, with good search facilities so that the social worker can skim through the file easily, straight language rather than codes, easy entry at any point and some facilities to give it an edge over traditional files. Extra space would be needed in social work offices for desktop computers or terminals, but much room currently used for storing folders would be vacated. The most likely way client files would be stored is on disks, probably the smaller floppy ones, about the size of a 45 r.p.m. record. One floppy disk would hold at least two substantial case files in all their detail, possibly more, so overall office space needs for files would be much less than at present. While there would need to be a central file equivalent to a card index, and probably also a single resource store, to permit client checks, there is no reason why detailed case material should be available outside each social work office. This would involve preparing, updating and preserving computer files in the local office, and so have implications for the sort of work done by clerical staff. Certainly there would have to be some investment in training, but the extent of tasks would not justify any fall in clerical employment.

It is easier to present the case for and against a dual system than a single computer system because we have experience of the former, whereas the latter remains in the realm of future possibilities, with some inevitable surprises and unforeseen snags. The reader may well be sensible to retain a degree of cynicism, but may also have to keep an awareness of the rolling band-wagon impact of computing on modern industrial society. A historical overview does suggest that the dual system into which most agencies have entered is a first stage, a modification of traditional approaches and part of an organic progress to new arrangements. It is, therefore, a passing phase which may move slowly, but is nevertheless gradually making way for the next stage. On the basis of experience to date the question – Does computerisation work in our personal social services? – gets a mixed answer. The theory of computing may be logical and predictable, but reality throws up teething problems, unexpected snags, extra work, limits to the usefulness of computer output and some very tricky issues of principle. Yet discussions with social workers suggested that while many shared these frustrations and reservations, especially a suspicion about threats to confidentiality, most of those who had the opportunity to use a computer system welcomed it, and a small majority considered it to be helpful for social workers as well as managers. Even if the only facility currently available for the practitioner is to check on clients and resources, this is seen as a big advance on the old system of ringing around numerous offices in an attempt to pick up bits of information.

The experience for social workers to date is one of contributing to a management information system, and getting a few useful goodies in return. The big expansion in benefits for the practitioner is for the future, and not necessarily the distant future. A lot will depend on whether the money and will is there to give social work practice a boost. The technical potential already exists, and the next chapter will suggest what could be offered in the next few years.

8

Keying in Social Work Practice

This chapter is not intended as speculation – whether about political and economic developments – or about technological progress. Rather it aims to set out realistic prospects for the next few years – up to the end of the 1880s – or, if economic circumstances continue to apply a brake, into the 1990s. General developments in computing will have a useful impact on the economic situation, because there is no reason to predict an end to cheaper equipment. In relation to their capabilities computers have fallen massively in price, perhaps by as much as a factor of 10 times over the last decade. The reasons are a mixture of technological and production factors – ever more efficient processing circuits, smaller size needing less raw materials, the benefits of mass production and substantial competition between manufacturers.

Peripheral gadgets – printers, disk drives, screens, modems and so forth – have become cheaper, but to a lesser extent. It is a little misleading to give actual prices, but at present (mid-1984) a useful micro-computer with printer, screen and disk drive can be bought for less than £2000, while £20 000 will cover a linked system for six social workers, each having a keyboard and screen, with shared storage and printer. Prices continue to fall, but local authorities are not necessarily good at getting best value for money in their computer purchasing. They tend to have long-standing relationships with traditional computer manufacturer/suppliers, and the equipment of firms like IBM is more expensive than equivalents from other companies. The major world producers of computer equipment are America and Japan, but there is a British industry (such as ICL, Sinclair and Acorn), so a 'Buy British' policy is possible.

As well as getting cheaper, computers are smaller and much more powerful than their predecessors, and this is another trend likely to continue. The size of equipment is already well within a scale appropriate to sitting on without wholly taking up a desk top, and portable sets are coming on to the market. The next few years will probably see quite a development of portable, battery-driven equipment, including some that can be plugged into or even fitted in a car. This will give social workers the capacity to carry file data around, make entries at short notice and do tasks like welfare benefits assessments on home visits.

The extra power of computers is partly a straightforward matter of more memory capacity, and partly an increase in internal flexibility. This latter in particular is a useful development because it can further the process of making the computer more approachable. Achieving more 'user-friendliness' is primarily the result of internal programming, which in turn demands more of the memory capacity. If more memory is used for internal purposes, less is available for the user to fill with such as case-files. Any development which increases overall memory (even if it is an issue solely for smaller computers) will aid the quantitative storage needs of social workers. Greater power will also show as faster work, though processing speeds are already so speedy that many people would not notice the difference.

A problem which manufacturers have not yet tackled is that of the incompatibility of different makes and models of computers. Japanese micro-computer makers have announced the intention of ensuring that programs written and run on one type of machine can be used on others, but for the most part machines are not capable of handling material generated on different sorts of equipment. This could become a nuisance, especially as industry has a poor record of coming to grips with this kind of issue – note how many decades it has taken to standardise even something as basic as a mains electric plug. It may not affect social workers, but it could if, for example, someone starts doing an assessment on the office computer and then wants to finish it in the evening on the home computer.

Home computers represent an effective and growing opportunity for social workers to acclimatise to computing. Several of those who were asked for their views on computers had home experience, and a large majority had children who used computers at school, spouses who used them at work, or both. The wider community context of computing experiences, especially through schools, is likely to serve as a helpful environment for developments in the personal social services. This will be reinforced by the extent to which professionals from other services – doctors, solicitors and teachers, for example – are incorporating computer processes into their own activities. Indeed, in a few years it will be the social work office without computing facilities that will stand out as unusual and unprogressive.

The extension of computing into social work practice will not be the result of a revolutionary new approach. It is important to keep in mind that the basis of practice usage is the same as for management, and that is a dependable and up-to-date client information store. Most (though not all) developments will have their origins in the client files, backed up by resource files. Most of the suggestions from social workers about the new computer services they would like to see were enlargements and refinements of the existing systems, with a particular emphasis on easing the administrative load of front-line staff. In a survey of social workers in Cornwall the question 'What do workers see as potential areas for computerisation?' provoked answers about setting up community resource files (including the private and voluntary sectors), getting more detailed and topical information about the availability of resources and using the computer to help with 'procedures' (Whaley, 1983, pp. 34–5). The remainder of the chapter will follow through these and other ideas for the immediate future.

Individual case-files

It has already been pointed out that there is no technical difficulty about transferring the entire contents of a case-file to the computer, and this is the essential first step for further developments. Quite literally this means that what currently goes into a folder – forms, reports, notes, reviews, all of it – is entered through a keyboard and stored on (probably) a small floppy disk. To the extent to which manual files are handwritten there will be additional typing work. Diagrams (such as a body outline showing injury points for a victim of child abuse) can be included. There may be some advantages in having a specially written program to do these tasks, but there are already numerous 'off-the-shelf' micro-computer packages which would be suitable for a trial, mostly involving word-processing activity.

Once the client file is on computer there are two clear routes to considering what can be done next. One is to look at the program that is being used, to see what useful facilities it offers. The second is to note the uses of traditional manual files, to see how far the computerised version can match or improve on them,

Obviously a purpose-written program can be structured to do a range of tasks, but a conventional word-processing package from the local computer shop will be far from useless. Just about the cheapest on the market is the program being used for this book, so the illustration which follows is from the lower end of the sophistication range.

The program is called Quill, and it functions on a Sinclair QL computer. All entries are typed in through a conventional typewriter keyboard, and simultanously displayed on a screen (either a standard TV or a higher resolution monitor, which gives a clearer picture). Once material is entered it can be stored for future use on small cartridges, less common than floppy disks, but doing the same kind of job. The cartridges simply slot into the computer, and each one will hold about 15 000 words. Clear instructions on how to use the program can be shown on the screen at any time, so if a social worker wants to make an entry rather than leave it to a clerical colleague, there is no difficulty.

Files can be structured in the computer in a variety of ways to suit whatever the social worker or agency prefers. Documents can be entered in any order and shuffled around at will, and each can be identified by label, title, page number or document number. Draft material, such as the first version of a report, can be typed in and then revised, corrected and licked into shape, using a number of facilities for editing. Material can be added or deleted at any time.

An existing file is loaded into the computer from a cartridge, and any part of it can be displayed. This can be done by scrolling through to have a quick view of the whole file, stopping as desired, instructing the computer to display a particular page (a table of contents can list what is on each page), or, if the user is not sure where to look, asking the computer to find any document where a particular label (a name, for example) occurs. In short the program will do the equivalent of checking through a manual file, to review various bits or find specific entries. On the assumption that a printer is connected, a copy of the whole file or any particular document can be run off.

In addition Quill has a couple more useful skills. If, for example, a social worker has to produce a report, for a panel meeting or the Court, and wishes to incorporate chunks from documents on the file, then this can be done without writing them all out again. The edit facility can be used to help compose the report, slotting in phrases, sentences or paragraphs from other parts of the file. Then a computer command called 'Design' allows the social worker to print out the report in a variety of formats, as a letter, on whatever sizes of paper can be got into the printer or on a form. Pieces can be incorporated from more than one file, and two files can be merged, if the need ever arises.

These are the abilities of a mass-produced package which is included in the price of a £400 home computer. Even at this primitive level there are advantages over manual files. If we now move on to look at how we have or would like to use manual files, a range of new possibilities emerge which the computer can be programmed to handle. Part of the job of the social worker is to establish a structure of contacts with clients, whether resulting from casual arrangements, specific contracting or legally required supervision. The source of reminders for this work is the record on file and the social worker's diary, though some offices also have timetabling aids. The job may be done in a haphazard way, as and when the pressures of work permit, or it may be more carefully planned to take in both timetabling and such other factors as travel patterns. Computers can be programmed so that as soon as they are turned on in the morning they display any visits or contacts the social worker is required to make in this context. The computer can list those due today, or during the week or those overdue, and can go on nagging until it is told that a chore has been done. Indeed, there is nothing to stop a computer doing what BL have done for those who get into a car and forget to put on a seat belt – give a smooth-tongued message about it. The computer can easily give reminders for any regularly repeated task, or, once the data are entered, draw attention to any special features, such as birthdays. It will send birthday cards to all clients if the worker wants!

An initial phase in any work with a client is to undertake an assessment. Sometimes this is a unique process which requires a deal of thought and weighing up evidence before coming to conclusions and recommendations. On the other hand the assessment may be a rather more formalised chore, either because the agency has established a standardised procedure, or because a somewhat mechanistic aspect is present. This refers to the sorts of assessments which involve the use of priority scales, schedules for aids or point counts. Many social workers already spend a lot of time using formalised assessment procedures, and, because they are generally quicker to do than less structured approaches, they are becoming more common. An example is the assessment of an applicant for Part III accommodation, in which a known range of specific factors about the client and his/her circumstances is used to aid a recommendation, and where the conclusion is often about which category of priority to designate. Another illustration is the assessment of handicapped people, to establish a weighting which then features in the calculation of staffing needs in houses, hostels and training centres. Any form of assessment which is standardised and leads to a grading or points score relating to eligibility for a service can be handled through the computer both comprehensively and accurately. In the longer run, after trials, it should be possible for more complex assessments, like risk measurement, to be aided in the same way.

This is done by putting into the computer the process of assessment, along with weightings, special factors and any other nuances. As was explained in Chapter 5 when discussing the activities of programmers, the task begins by converting the assessment sequence into a flow chart which moves through all possible channels, takes in the required data and leads to end-points, in this context to recommendations. This is then rewritten as a computer program, with built-in gaps to be filled with information about the individual client being assessed. These gaps can be filled either by drawing the information direct from the client's computer file, or by asking questions on the screen for the user to type in the answers. In this application the computer is making calculations. It has been told to give greater weight or a higher score to one answer as compared to other possibilities, and it does so. Thus the computer may be told that in an application for housing for a homeless family a single parent with two children gets a higher score than a couple with one child, and it calculates and recommends accordingly. The computer is not, and will not for a few years, be able to make comparisons with how other cases have been treated, or draw interferences from other data which have passed through its memory. That is to say, it will not recommend that Mrs Smith is given a Part III place because Mrs Jones, who got one a couple of months ago, was in similar circumstances. This kind of potential is in the realms of artificial intelligence, which is currently under technological development, and will be touched on in the next chapter.

It is important to stress as well, both in relation to assessment and what comes later about decision-making, that the computer is not trying to challenge or take over the social worker's judgement. The computer will only do what it is told. There is a risk here, in that someone else could be doing the telling (a manager, for example), and this brings us back to the political situation. Leaving that aside, because it has already been discussed, the social worker can always decide not to use the computer, or can disregard the computer's recommendations. Perhaps the social worker should have reasonable grounds for making that choice, but the computer's word is not inviolable.

A computerised client file can be used in much the same way as a manual file to provide the social worker with the information needed for making decisions. The computer can be programmed to go further, by drawing the worker's attention to salient features of the case, and by feeding in relevant material drawn from a wider data-base. In outline the traditional process of making decisions about, say, a treatment plan, is to collect relevant information through the assessment, and then draw on professional judgement and experience to sort it all out. Other contributions may or may not come – through negotiations with the client, discussions with the team leader, studying theory or looking at research into the subject. The imperfections of the real world will also provoke a check on the availability of resources, an attempt to get approval, if needed, from on high and an evaluation of the client's ability to make reasonable use of the proposed counsels or services. The decisions which emerge may be the result of much agonising or widespread discussion, in a case conference for instance, or may be reached in an easy way. Computers can help by offering confirmation of the simple, and giving much-needed support for the really difficult decisions.

One level of support stems from the way the computer can be asked to handle the subject client file. Particularly if the file is a large one the worker needs to be able to extract vital bits, rather than trying to 'contain' the whole contents. The computer can help with this by being programmed to pull out sections which have been identified in the past as important (like 'tabbing' a manual file), or are requested by the user as the focus of a search. This sort of search says to the computer – go through the file and pull out all those documents where a particular word or phrase (say, for example, 'violent behaviour') is mentioned.

Alternatively the computer can be made to interact in an informative way with the social worker, by feeding it what Schoech and Schkade call 'Conversational software that allows the user a dialogue with the data base in familiar logic and language' (1980, p. 567). The salient information then comes forward on a question-and-answer basis, and within the confines of a limited vocabulary for questions from the worker the technology exists to voice rather than type them.

While the client file will form the core data-base for decision-making, there is a long and sometimes controversial history of trying to broaden the framework. Social workers do this naturally, every time they draw on experience. Others have tried to be more structured in offering comparative information about the way things worked out in other similar circumstances. The sensitive aspect of this approach concerns the formal use of an empirical method to collect data in format and volume so as to permit projections to be made, and in particular predictions about what decisions stand the best prospects of leading to successful outcomes. It is when the prediction runs counter to the social worker's own judgement that trouble starts, and arguments are made about the dangers of allowing systems of this kind to replace professional expertise. Earlier a soothing response was given, that if the social worker felt like it, the 'outside' recommendation could be ignored. There is a rather less compromising and more accurate retort when it comes to empirically proven predictive methods – if they can be shown to be more accurate than professional judgement in a sample of instances, they should take precedence. Professional judgement is not infallible.

Computers are well suited to be harnessed to this kind of activity. They are best at searching and sorting large quantities of material, and picking out the required items. They can be programmed to draw on a vast data-base to pick out similarities between cases, note the range of decisions which were made, and give a follow-up on the outcome of those decisions, if and when they were implemented. The computer can be passive or intrusive in doing this job. Schoech and Schkade's paper about a Decision Support System (DSS) in a child welfare agency leaves the initiative firmly with the social worker: 'The essential function of a DSS is to enhance the judgement of the decision maker at all stages of problem solving by allowing easy query of highly flexible and well managed groups of data pertinent to the situation.' (p. 568.) It is arguable that if the computer has information which really ought to be taken into account – perhaps something the social worker does not know about – it should be thrust forward and not wait to be requested.

Once individual client information is linked to a broader data-base (which might be taken to be the total office caseload) as an aid to decision-making, then one further computing activity becomes feasible. This is outcome evaluation. A computer can be asked to cross-reference data in numerous ways. These can include checking back on initial objectives to see how far they have been achieved, or to see what progress has been made in treatment (for example, goals or set tasks) initiated by the social worker. Moving outside the subject client's file, several more general outcomes can be measured, such as how often a recommended course of action can in practice be implemented, and if not why not; or how often, according to a designated set of criteria, a particular treatment is successful. In this way the computer could fill an important gap in social work knowledge, and do so routinely and continuously.

Composite data analysis

Already a number of developments originating from individual files have spilled over into composite material, perhaps containing the total office or team workload. For some agencies it is talking about the present rather than the future to note that a computer can do for a local office what it does for the agency – provide cumulative (usually statistical) analysis of the range of activities carried out by the office staff. There is not much that needs to be said about this, because it is in essence a small-scale version of a management information system. A relatively minor move forward, however, opens up an additional dimension, in that it can offer the individual social worker the opportunity to look at aspects of caseload management. Procedures already exist, some computerised, to indicate caseload sizes, drawing on complex weighting arrangements. These could be extended to incorporate a more dynamic element, such as the rate of turnover of clients, variations in anticipated work pressures, week by week, on the basis of known commitments and a contingency allocation for emergencies, or the most time-saving way of timetabling a set of tasks. An interactive program could also be written to aid a caseload review, such as that devised by Vickery (1977), or to monitor structured sequences with individual clients, such as task-setting, and relate then to a theoretical base. So the computer can help the thorny problem, a regular pain in the backside for social work students, of integrating theory and practice! The way the computer would do this is to have stored a model of a structured process, like a task-centred program or a behavioural sequence, as a basis for commenting on the use of such approaches with specific clients. Comments could be evaluative ('you're doing well so far'), time-keeping ('you won't finish in the three months you set yourself unless you speed up'), nagging ('you won't get your mentally handicapped client to clean his teeth on his own if you keep helping him') or theoretical ('you say your client wants to skip one task and go onto the next, but Reid says on this subject . . . .'). In this usage the computer can help the social worker to handle a caseload more efficiently and reflectively, and in so doing extend the worker's horizons beyond a preoccupation with the immediate pressures.

A further potential for the computer is to help trainee social workers, by making use of the computer's ability to contain and manipulate client information. It is not a big step to use such a program framework as the basis for setting up simulated material for use in training. One of the weaknesses of social work training is that the students go into practice placements, especially the first one, with insufficient preparation, and without their tutors or supervisors knowing whether it is safe to let them loose on clients. This is not a reflection on efforts to prepare students, which may be extensive, so much as on the gap between the detailed reality of the placement and the more general academic framework of the course syllabus. Many training courses already use video and other equipment to provide realistic illustration, facilitate simulation exercises or give back to students an impression of how they tackle the job. Computers can reinforce this, and an example is offered by Smith, Parmar and Paget (1980), who have experimented on a simulated reception interview with 'Elsie'. The setting for the student is: 'You are duty social worker in a general hospital with a waiting-room full of people. The receptionist reports a middle-aged woman is asking to see the social worker.' (p. 496.) The student has to decide what to do, and the computerised Elsie is programmed with enough flexibility to respond to the student.

Resource files

These are already a feature of many management information systems, and the initial round of new developments is likely to take the form of extending the data-base. In this context 'resource' has a broad definition, spanning from budgets, through places in residential and day-care centres, to foster parents, stocks of stationery and training opportunities. A paper from the chairman of the Hampshire DISP group on Personal Computing (himself a team leader in the area office) lists fifteen possible micro-computer applications, of which eight are for resource files (Hardman, 1984).

A comment made earlier supported the view that resource files would generally need to be centralised, covering the whole agency. The reason is that many resources are not solely at the disposal of a single office, and often need careful allocation among competing demands. There are, however, purely localised resources, and it is a matter of convenience whether they are held separately and locally or merged with general files. Unlike client records, the issue here is less fraught because confidentiality is not so vital. For organisational purposes some categorisation of an extended resource information system is feasible:

1. Resources serving the whole agency, and covered by an agency-wide allocation procedure. This will include residential homes, day-care and training centres, and some specialised facilities.

2. a. Agency resources or budgets which can only be used with approval from HQ.

b. Out-of-agency resources, also needing sanction from HQ. Normally this will only contain items which have to be paid for.

3. Resources which are allocated to local areas (usually annually), but subject to ceilings on use. This may include budgets for telephones or aids and adaptations.

4. Resources for staff development, again usually centrally allocated, by management or a training section.

5. Community services and resources developed directly by the agency, such as foster parents, potential adoptive parents and adult placements.

6. Agency services which are normally handled at the local level, for example home helps and intermediate treatment facilities.

7. Resources belonging to or shared with other statutory agencies in the area, and used in the context of multi-disciplinary activity.

8. Private and voluntary resources, both local and regional. This could range from lists of individual volunteers who can be called on when needed, through to private nursing homes and voluntary service agencies.

9. Emergency resources. This might include the well-known emergency services and also resources which can be called on for special or unusual emergencies – the 24-hour-a-day plumber, temporary overnight shelter or duty dentist. This is a file which could be shared with other agencies.

10. A resource data-base for meeting requests for information and advice about the personal social services, other components of the welfare state, voluntary services or local resources. This is potentially a file which could be shared and stretched almost endlessly.

11. Support service resources, such as stationery, office equipment, furniture and so forth. The file could also include information on service contracts, guarantees, when overhauls become due and when items were bought or might need replacing.

12. Current and capital budgets for the agency, including estimates and projections. Proposals for agency developments, with papers for discussion. Committee agendas and minutes, with comparable information about management team meetings.

Current research and field trials, and developments in front-line settings. In short, this would be an internal communication file which would move beyond lists of resources into plans and ideas about future resource developments.

This list is not exhaustive, but it is long and varied enough to show that there is enormous scope for growth in information about agency and other local resources. The next question concerns what, from a social worker's angle, should be on these files. Much of this is obvious – size, location, purpose, preferred users, general and special characteristics, rules for use, procedures for getting access and so forth. A social worker will need the computer file to be able to display all the information pertinent to assessing the appropriateness of the resource for a particular client or circumstance. There are a couple of more sensitive aspects. One concerns qualitative material. There are many resources used by social workers which will be evaluated less through factual description and more by 'feel', atmosphere or staff personality. A regularly occurring example is when a worker is trying to find a foster home or a residential place, and is wanting to match foster parents or residential staff to the client. Should the computer file stick to facts and figures, or should it include a wider range of material, some of it more subjective? This is one facet of resource computing which does raise issues of confidentiality, and there may be a justifiable policy decision to exclude such information simply to avoid having to shroud the whole file in secrecy. On the other hand atmospheric and personality comments are as important in relation to the resource as they are about the client, and computers can handle restricted access segments to a file. Even so this begs the question of the impact on an agency of comments, sometimes critical ones, about members of staff being placed on file and viewed by other staff. We are prepared to do it about people on the fringes (like foster parents), but draw the line at salaried colleagues. Are we pussy-footing, or is it good ethics?

A more acute difficulty stems from the imbalance between demand and supply of many resources, which in practical terms means that too often a resource is fully used, and when a vacancy occurs the social worker has to be persuasive and sharp to get hold of it. Waiting lists cope with some of these problems, but workers will be well aware that queues are there to be jumped; in any event very scarce places in residential and day-care settings are not usually filled simply by reference to a waiting list – a case has to be made for each applicant. How can the computer help here? In the first place the computer can do nothing unless its files are kept up to date, but if they are it can be used to communicate opportunities about scarce resources to social workers. It can also be used to advertise underused resources (if there are such things!). Both of these are simply a matter of getting on to the resource file that a vacancy exists, when it came up, when it will be filled and whether any special factors will apply. Obviously it is no use entering the vacancy so late that it has already been filled.

This is about as far as existing computerised resource files have developed, but it only goes part way to solving the problem because it still leaves the social worker, or someone else in the office, the chore of scouring the whole file to see if any spaces have been notified. In practice resource files tend to be by-passed and other ways are found to get the latest news. A simple process to overcome this is to use the computer in much the same way as was suggested for reminders about client contacts the social worker should be making. Every morning, as the computer is switched on, it is programmed to make an automatic run through the resource data and display any changes, or note solely those changes which indicate a vacancy. The implication for the other end of the computer, where the resource file is created, is that changes must be entered with as much frequency. A slightly more flexible approach would be to display changes as and when they are entered, so that whenever a social worker's screen is not being used for something else, the latest state of resources is shown.

A rather more fundamental use for the computer is to alter the sequence of events. For example, in seeking a place in an old people's home for an elderly client, the social worker starts by building up a picture of the client, to aid the initial decision, and to narrow down the type of home that would be suitable. At about the same time a formal application is likely to be prepared, not necessarily for a specific place so much as to establish general eligibility. The social worker then has to keep checking vacancies and decide, on each occasion, whether to push forward that client for the selection panel or whatever allocation process is used. At the other end of the scene an old people's home finds itself with a vacancy, which is then notified, and the procedure to fill it is initiated. The staff of the home are unlikely to get the opportunity to state in detail the sort of person they would like, though they may have a negative power of veto over any proposed person who they considered unsuitable. An alternative computerised sequence could be for the social worker to do the initial assessment and check on eligibility as before, and then to enter client particulars on the computer, along with a statement of the type of resources being sought. At the other end when a vacancy occurs in a home the staff initiate notification to the computer, along with a description of who they would find best suited to fill it. Two routes then open up. Either a member of staff (residential, HQ or whoever is designated) can look at client profiles, link them to the details of the vacancy and invite a number of clients' names to go forward. Or the computer can take the two sets of data, client profiles and resource vacancy description, undertake matching and suggest suitable placements.

The illustration is about residential care, but the processes discussed have a much wider relevance, including placements in the community. Indeed the idea of circulating a client profile has already been put into practice in the way some agencies advertise for foster parents. An important point to keep in mind about the role of the computer is that it can be programmed to undertake matching (it already has a somewhat dubious record in computer dating!), and without necessarily using its recommendations the procedure allows suggestions to be drawn to the social worker's attention.

Repetitive tasks and calculations

The subject areas intended to be covered by this title are some administrative chores, especially form-filling; some of the more standardised aspects of work with clients, like Part III assessments; and tasks involving complex calculations, like benefits eligibility. Much has already been said on these topics, and this section aims at little more than drawing together earlier comments.

Some aspects are not contentious, and computerisation would be widely accepted. This would certainly include a speedier means of form-filling. Social work offices tend to be full of forms, application forms, notification forms, forms about forms, all of them printed on paper and waiting to be filled in. Almost all of them are not filled from original data, but by extracting bits from existing sources, commonly the client file. The computer could gobble up this kind of task. It could contain in store copies of all forms with reference numbers for identification, either with the potential to have the form itself printed if needed, or so that it knows what answers have to go where on the form. This latter opens up the option of putting a blank form in the printer and telling the computer to fill it in. Given the computer's ability to search for and cross-reference information, it would be able to draw from its data sources the material to fill in the required form, either for transmission to the printer, or direct visual passage to anywhere else on the computer network. If the data are not available on file to answer a particular question on the form then the computer can display a request for help.

Another welcomed ability is in handling welfare benefits assessments. Experience to date has shown that this is not as easy a task as was first thought, but the next few years will undoubtedly see the problems overcome. The difficulties stem in part from the complexities of the welfare benefits system itself, and the challenge they present to the programmer. More persistent trouble is likely to arise from continual changes to the system and areas of discretion. In theory changes are not difficult to handle. If the sums to be paid out for specific benefits are increased or the detailed rules for eligibility are altered, the program can be suitably modified. In practice if changes come too thick and fast the program will spend a lot of time out of commission while alterations are being written and de-bugged. The welfare benefits system is not stable enough for easy computing.

The use of discretion, for example, over whether or not a particular set of circumstances constitute eligibility, does not fit comfortably into the computer. Precedent can be incorporated, providing it has something of the status of a new rule, as it tends to in legal practice; but arbitrariness is a different matter. All the computer can do then is to note the boundaries within which decisions are made, and suggest alternative calculations along the lines of – if decision *A* is taken then the benefit payable will be . . . but if the decision is *B* then the benefit will be less or nothing at all. The computer could be helpful, through its ability to review previous comparable situations, in suggesting when an appeal against a decision would be justifiable.

If social workers are happy about a computer helping with welfare benefits calculations then it is likely to be because they feel unable or unwilling to do the job themselves. Some will say they haven't the skill, knowledge or numeracy, while others may assert that it is not a proper social work task. In theory there is no real difference between the process of checking benefits eligibility and Part III eligibility – both are calculations based on facts, with a component of judgement. Why then are social workers likely to be so content to use the computer for the former and so suspicious about a similar approach to the latter? Is it solely that one is impossibly complex to handle manually, but not the other?

There is an issue here about what decisions are so crucially a matter of professional judgement that they should not be handled in any other way. The solution is beyond the scope of this book, though it is appropriate to make the mischevous suggestion that social workers may be willing to abandon the principle if the job itself is too complicated or tedious. Why can one client's material living standards be left to the computer, while another's must get individual personal attention? Is it perhaps not an issue of principle at all, but instead a matter of using the computer as and when it demonstrates its utility? Whatever the position, it needs to be noted that any computer which can handle the vast size, complexity and fluctuations of the welfare benefits scene would have no difficulty with smaller repetitive jobs like home-help eligibility, or identifying the nearest relative under the terms of the 1983 Mental Health Act (the author has written a program to do this), or ensuring that all necessary steps have been taken in handling a child abuse referral. Within the state of current technology any process which is standardised enough to be expressible as a flow chart can be dealt with on a computer.

A similar area of social work activity involves the use of standardised tests or measurements, where again structured processes are being employed to achieve a desired end. Once more there is possible professional controversy over the value of such activities (like IQ tests); but once more they are, if wanted, suitable for computing.

General trends

The previous sections have suggested ways in which the computer could encroach into social work practice, quite quickly if the money is found for equipment and programmers. None of the applications are beyond widely available technology. The social worker reader may have been excited by the prospects, but may (more likely?) have found them distasteful and threatening. Certainly the hope has been that the reader would turn back and think again about the broader political and ethical context within which these developments might take place, because cumulatively their impact on the social worker could be substantial.

As soon as computers are installed, and pressure or temptation builds up to use them, the whole of social work practice risks lurching towards a more structured and standardised approach to tasks. Certain activities will feel easier because they are on the same wavelength as the computer, in the same way that some views and actions already come more willingly because they are known to command management approval. In contrast, just as a social worker will hesitate, and perhaps feel some stress, before acting in a way which challenges agency policy or practice, so will going against the computer become a source of controversy. The sorts of qualities to be lost in this process are much like those threatened by the extension of bureaucracy – individual flair, intuition, imagination and experimentation (see Glastonbury, Cooper and Hawkins, 1983, chapter 3, for further discussion in relation to bureaucracy). Certain established methods of social work intervention – such as behaviourism – will also be supported, while others will fit less comfortably. As a general comment, it seems likely that increased computerisation will support the trend to favour the shorter-term and more controllable methods of using social worker time.

Much will depend on how the computer is pushed on to the scene. The nightmare for social workers, as already mentioned and dismissed, is that the computer will become the tool through which managers establish ever-present control over the minutiae of day-to-day work. This is the 'Is Big Brother Watching You?' fear (see Powell, 1980). Yet if that is too extravagant an expectation, there are risks of more subtle moves in the same direction, not necessarily towards direct managerial control so much as towards an atmosphere in which the computer rules. At root will be the extent to which the social worker's computer comes to be seen as the depository of what is right, both in the sense of what is professionally correct and agency approved. Some scenes come to mind. A harassed team leader is approached by an inexperienced social worker for help in deciding on a course of action: 'Sorry. I haven't got time to go into it. Go and see what the computer suggests.' An edict goes round the office to the effect that 'Well-proven guidelines for handling child abuse cases are contained in the computer. Any social worker who wishes to act in a way which runs counter to the guidelines must place a memo on file explaining the reasons for this decision.' These risks are minimised if the computer can be fully and firmly incorporated into the framework of professional judgement, so that a part of that judgement concerns when to use and when not to use the computer. In the past new technology has intervened (like tape recorders), and have been integrated by some, ignored by others. Social workers have not been very good at latching on to new gadgets, but until the right political decisions have been made there may be good sense in treating computer developments circumspectly. Resistance may well be needed to get a reasonable sense of pacing into computerisation, unless the economic climate continues to do the job. A feature of the technological revolution is precisely that it has been a revolution with an extremely fast rate of development and innovation. In any widespread sense computer applications have fallen well behind technical potential, and this has probably been necessary to protect society from the upheaval of too fast a rate of change.

How will change affect the social worker? In the debate about the possible role of computers in reducing employment, the choice in social work has been to see two stark extremes. Either the computer will replace the social worker, and social service – like the telephone and other public services before it – will push computers into the front line. Or the computer will take all those boring repetitive jobs away from social workers and leave them free to concentrate on the really important and difficult tasks, which can only be handled with traditional social work skills. Speculating between these poles would be delving into fantasy, and in any event the computer is hardly likely to be in a position to take over for decades to come. The more immediate issue arises from the ability the computer already has to do humble tasks, and perhaps as a result increase the proportion of a social worker's time spent on 'difficult' activities and client contacts. We know that these aspects of the job can be stressful, and that 'burn-out' is a concept applicable to social work practice. We suspect, but have little precise data, that routine tasks need to be interspersed with client contacts, in order to help the social worker cope with the stressful content of the role. If there is a balance here it will be important to monitor the impact of the computer to ensure that the balance is not tipped in a damaging direction. More time to spend with clients may only be desirable and sensible from the viewpoint of those who do not have to see clients at all, or have relatively unstressful jobs.

In conclusion this chapter will draw on one of the few documented experiments into the computer's role in social work practice, in order to reiterate a view stated several times already: 'Computer applications if left solely to managers will primarily serve the needs of managers. If the applications are to become a tool for caseworkers, caseworkers must become involved in the agency's computerization efforts from the very beginning.' (Schoech and Schkade, 1980, p. 573.)

9

The Robot Social Worker

Abels tells a story about Mrs X and the social work computer. She comes to the office asking for aid, gives some information and a few moments later gets a calculation of her benefits entitlement. Shortly afterwards the cheque pops out of a slot. Mrs X has also talked about personal problems, and the computer recommends that she join a group starting the next day. At the same time reports of previous contacts with the client are pouring in from all round the country, with printed copies for any human staff who may be in the office. During the group meeting Mrs X is asked to keep her hand on a plate on the arm of her chair, so that a computer can read and analyse her electrical impulses. And so it goes on, until Mrs X finishes up with a regular cheque, support, satisfaction and a job. When asked how she felt about being counselled by a computer she said: 'I thought there was a social worker at the other end of that machine typing answers.' (Abels, 1972, pp. 5–6.)

This is the fantasy of the enthusiast, that the computer can be so human-like that the client is fooled. It is the dream of **R2D2** and **C3P0**, robots with a heart and mind, and the touching attractiveness of emotion and fallibility. But does it bear any resemblance to what might happen in the future? The idea of a visible robot, in the sense of a tin social worker or a benevolent Dalek, can be ignored. There is no purpose for it, and the computer shop front will be the keyboard, microphone or slot to receive and dispense documents. There will still be office staff (humans that is!), more in the background, and the client of the future might not expect to see any of them, except possibly a receptionist. We can certainly expect the computer to encroach more and more between the client and worker, but not necessarily to replace the traditional relationship. To some extent the computer may protect the social worker, who will be able to hide behind it when an unwanted client is reported in the waiting-room, and exercise some choice about whom to see and when. This need be no cause of guilt because by the time it happens we shall all be used to dealing with computers, almost wherever we go. Banks are already showing the way, with Cashpoint centres and the like. The important factor, however, is not that the computer will have more success in becoming human-like, but that it will do certain tasks more reliably and quickly than humans.

In discussing the future of computers we are covering communications as well as computing, and what has been written so far in this chapter is mainly about the former. Indeed C. Evans (1979) feels we should look even more widely, to see what broader world circumstances will influence the priorities in computer developments. He cites as an example (in Chapter 8) the potential computers have to respond to world shortages of wood pulp by dispensing altogether with the printed word. After all, the entire reading needed for a social work qualifying course could be accommodated on a few computer memory chips. It is very difficult to judge how far such predictions are pure fantasy, and if not, just how they would impinge on social work.

One important argument developed by C. Evans (chapter 9), and repeated in public statements by Sir Clive Sinclair, is that those professions which have thrived by surrounding themselves with mystifying jargon and exclusive procedures will decline. We shall not, they argue, need to go to solicitors to get enlightenment on the law, or architects to get a range of possible designs for a home extension. The computer will call up mass-media services to do it all for us, while we recline in an armchair. Social work is much less at risk here. In the first place it is a profession which has made strenuous efforts through the 1970s and 1980s to dispense with mystification, despite its flirtation with systems theory. More importantly, it is a profession which deals less in facts and knowledge and more in helping to overcome human distress. So many social work skills are beyond the capacity of computers, even into the distant future.

The computer will continue to improve on its ways of enhancing social work practice, helping to make it more efficient and dependable. In particular we can look for a focus on the outcomes of different forms of intervention, through a growing sophistication in predictive techniques, and the development of projections. This latter refers to the prospect that the computer will be able to analyse a client's assessment data, and then project the likely results of a range of possible interventions. The projected scenarios could be used by worker or client to aid decision-making. Trying to work out the best choice from a number of options is a game we all play, and one which becomes vitally important when major life decisions are involved, like whether or not to take a child into care. With its grasp of client information and history, combined with a knowledge of present and probable future resources, as well as portraits of foster parents and residential staff, the computer will have a sound database. Add to this an ability to analyse the outcomes of many previous situations of a similar kind, and the computer begins to have a broader frame of reference than the social worker. Throw in the possibility that the worker is feeling tired, under pressure and generally fed up, and the client might actually prefer to have the computer suggest some solutions.

Another certainty for the future is that we shall all have to change our understanding of AI. The A = Artificial can remain, but I for Insemination must be abandoned in favour of I = Intelligence. The next generation of computers – that is, the computers for the 1990s – will boast artificial intelligence. In essence AI will reflect an ability to break out of certain frontiers limiting computer functioning; in practice it will, for many years, mean no more than stretching those boundaries a little. At present one set of boundaries controls data going into the computer. Regardless of how smooth and easy the communication becomes, the modern computer can only take in what it is formally given. We have to make entries. We cannot leave the computer to pick up its own material, though we can tell it how, once it has received information, to keep what is useful and discard what is not. One aspect of AI is to get beyond the need to make an entry to the computer, and conceptually this is the equivalent of endowing the machine with senses, both to see and hear (touch and smell as well?), and to interpret what it perceives. The first stage of any development in this direction is likely to be to give the computer the ability to absorb whatever data come into its orbit, to be considered and sorted later. We already have applications of this principle, for example with video cameras on motorways, filming randomly for later analysis to see if any offence shows up. This is part of the Big Brother image, but it presupposes a lot of little men in a back room going through the pictures for the tell-tale bits. It is hardly machine intelligence, and not likely to become so until the computer can, in this illustration, identify the snippets of behaviour which are against the law.

Social work already seems to be too weighed down with information, so a development which gathers still more may not be welcomed. However, there are some possible applications. The computer could, for example, listen in to an interview, record it in full, and then provide a summary. Certainly the ability to receive through a microphone rather than a keyboard will give much more flexibility for data intake. It will also of course engender much greater suspicion and distrust of the computer as a snooper.

The other boundaries of computing relate to the way data is used, once it is stored. Again there will not be any development which gives the computer an independent intelligence to work on this material, but there can be much more complex programming. The current frontier which is central to this aspect of AI is that a computer can only do what it is told. It cannot use initiative or decide to disobey – these are nonsensical concepts in computing. Closely allied is another boundary: that the computer can only be told to do certain things. It can be told to sort, search, do complex mathematics, draw pictures, but it cannot be told to use its imagination or its common sense. It hasn't got any. The initial phase in the development of AI in this context is likely to be extending the range of requests that can be made and acted on, and specifically to make it possible to give rather more general instructions than is the case at present. An illustration might clarify the point. Let us take a detailed computerised social history of a client who has been on the books for many years, and who has a long record of overdosing. Suppose we want to know if the incidents are showing any seasonal pattern, perhaps related to anniversaries. In the reasonably near future we should be able to say (or type) to the computer that we want the file searched for any reference to the words 'suicide' or 'overdose', and a print out of such references, with the sentence in which they appear and the date. We can also get hypotheses like the possible link to anniversaries checked out. We may get an accurate response, but because we have had to give precise instructions we may end up with some false incidents, for example because the computer has picked up a discussion on suicide rather than a report of an event. We may also miss some events because we have not asked for other possible wordings, like 'taking a bottle of aspirin'. The move into AI might help us to get a more useful response because we will be able to ask the computer in a more general way to search through for events involving taking an overdose. Instead of asking the computer to recognise words (often called 'key' words) we can ask it to recognise key ideas.

'Similarity' is another concept which the development of AI may help. At present, as far as the computer is concerned, similarity has either to be defined as 'the same as', or the characteristics which amount to similarity have to be precisely entered. We are asking the computer to use the notion of similarity when, for example, we want it to search the files for previous experiences similar to a case we are trying to resolve at present. The hope for AI is that it will be able to get the computer a little nearer to our own attitude to similarity when we are drawing on our experience, or looking around for comparisons. In practice our minds look not just for total similarity, but also for approximations or selected point of comparison. Furthermore we can then draw inferences from these approximations, and inferences are much more flexible than calculations. AI is very much concerned with the ability of the computer to infer. For example, tell a computer that a middle-aged single woman has been living for many years with an elderly dependent parent, and the computer will duly record it. Tell a social worker, and the prospect is there of inferring that perhaps the woman has endured deprivations and made many personal sacrifices. This is a rather simplistic inference, which certainly underrates the intelligence of the social worker, but it does serve to focus on the lack of intelligence of the computer. Yet even if AI gives us a little computer ability to infer, it is most unlikely to be of much value to social work practice. Inference is a major and complex skill in social work, primarily concerned with the ability to see between the lines and below the surface, to distinguish the superficial from the profound. This is not within the scope of computers.

Leaving AI there is one further practical impact of information technology on social workers and many others which should be noted. Specifically it relates to developments in communications which are already beginning to make it possible for people to work from home. 'Going to the office', indeed the office itself, may be nearing the end of its life. Instead people will stay at home to work, preferably in some desirable rural spot, and, in the jargon 'telecommute'. A report about its growth in America says that 'there's a seductiveness about it that seems irresistible and the signs are that it is heading for Britain' (Chris Rowley, *The Times*, 1 May 1984). No doubt the first beneficiaries will be managers, who can work at home because their entire job would otherwise be in an office block. Social workers, who have to make home visits, and be on hand to see people, could not take such advantage. However, social work began from home, and the first social workers did not have an office to go to. Many old child care officers and NSPCC workers will be able to recall from personal experience the filing cabinet and telephone in the front room. Change the cabinet for a computer terminal and the picture is much the same.

Is there a final word for social workers? Should it be of reassurance that the inevitable growth of computation will have primarily beneficial effects? Or should it be a warning to man the barricades, but be ready to face defeat? Who knows! One thing is certain, and that is that social workers will gain in proportion to their efforts now to influence the way the new technology is introduced. As Abels wrote prophetically in 1972: 'If we can determine some of the criteria for using computers in our work and develop a system of values for its use, the computer itself may be able to help us decide when to use it and when to use real people' (p. 11). It is inconceivable that the problems which clients bring to social workers could ever be sorted out in the total absence of 'real people', simply because their solution requires a sensitivity and perceptiveness which no computer could ever attain. The vital position to secure is that social workers play a full part in making policies and decisions about when and how to use computers in our personal social services.

Bibliography

Abels, P. (1972) 'Can Computers Do Social Work?', *Social Work*, 17, September.

Adler, M. and du Feu, D. (1977) 'Technical Solutions to Social Problems', *Journal of Social Policy*, 6.

Barclay, P. M. (1982) *Social Workers: their role and tasks*, Report of a Working Party chaired by P. M. Barclay, London, Bedford Square Press.

Boyd, L. H., Hylton, J. H. and Price, S. V. (1978) 'Computers in Social Work Practice: a review', *Social Work*, 23, September.

Briar, S. (1973) 'The Age of Accountability', *Social Work*, 18, January.

Brier, A. and Robinson, I. (1974) *Computers and the Social Sciences*, London, Hutchison.

British Association of Social Workers (Birmingham) (1972) *Confidentiality*, (1975) *A Code of Ethics for Social Work*, (1980) *Clients are Fellow Citizens*, and (1983) *Effective and Ethical Recording*.

Chapman, R. L. (1976) *The Design of Management Information Systems for Mental Health Organisations: a primer*, Rockville, Md, National Institute of Mental Health.

Community Information Project (1984) *Computer Factsheet* and (1984) *Computanews*.

Derbyshire, M. E. (1974) *A Comparison of Five Computerised Information Systems in Social Services Departments*, Lancashire County Social Services Department.

Dery, D. (1981) *Computers in Welfare: the MIS-match*, Beverly Hills and London, Sage.

Eason, M. (1982) 'Computerising Clients' Records', *Community Care*, 10 June.

Ebstein, J. (1984) 'New Technology; New Entitlement' – unpublished but reported in *The Guardian*, 13 August.

Evans, C. (1979) (1980) *The Mighty Micro*, London, Gollancz and Coronet. Page references are to the Coronet edition.

Evans, W. (1979) *Going On-line: a discussion document* and *Going On-line: discussion document III*, Winchester, both Hampshire County Social Services Department, respectively April and November 1979.

Fry, T. F. (1978) *Beginner's Guide to Computers*, Feltham, Newnes.

George, F. H. (1977) *Machine Takeover*, Oxford, Pergamon Press.

Glastonbury, B., Cooper, D. M. and Hawkins, P. (1983) *Social Work in Conflict*, Birmingham, British Association of Social Workers.

Goldberg, E. M. and Warburton, R. W. (1979) *Ends and Means in Social Work*, London, Allen & Unwin.

Gruber, M. (1974) 'Total Administration', *Social Work*, 19, September.

Hampshire County Social Services Department (1974) *Report of Computer Development Group* and *First Report on the Introduction of a Divisional Computer-based Information System*, Winchester.

Hardman, D. M. (1984) 'Microcomputer Applications', unpublished memorandum.

Hayman, M. (1980) 'Disabled and Administration Share the Rewards', *Practical Computing*, vol. 3, no. 6.

Healey, M. (1976) *Minicomputers and Microprocessors*, London, Hodder & Stoughton.

HMSO (1978) *Social Services Teams*, London, HMSO.

Hoshino, G. (1982) 'Computers: tool of management and social work practice', *Administration in Social Work*, vol. 5, no. 3/4.

Hoshino, H. and McDonald, T. P. (1975) 'Agencies in the Computer Age', *Social Work*, 20, January.

Hunt, R. and Shelley, J. (1979) *Computers and Commonsense*, Englewood Cliffs, NJ, Prentice-Hall.

LaMendola, W. (1982) 'Feasibility as a Consideration in Small Computer Selection', *Administration in Social Work*, vol. 5, no. 3/4.

LAMSAC (1982) *Survey of Local Authority Social Services Computer Applications*.

Leake, A. (1984) *Children at Risk: guidelines*, Department of Social Work Studies, Southampton University; and London, Borough of Merton Social Services Department.

Lewin. D. (1972) *Theory and Design of Digital Computers*, London, Nelson.

Lovelace, A. A. (1961) 'Notes' on Charles Babbage's Analytical Engine, first appearing in the *Biliothèque Universelle de Genève*, no. 82 (1842), and reprinted in Morrison, P. and E. (eds), *Charles Babbage and his Calculating Engines*, New York, Dover Publications.

Lynes, T. (1982) 'Benefit Printout', *New Society*, 9 December.

NALGO (1984) *The Personal Social Services*, London, National Association of Local Government Officers.

Parker, R. A. (1966) *Decision in Child Care*, London, Allen & Unwin.

Pascoe, N. (1978) *Social Services Information Project*, Research Memorandum 541, London, Greater London Council.

Payne, M. (1979) *Power, Authority and Responsibility in Social Services*, London, Macmillan.

Phillips, B. A., Dimsdale, B. and Taft, E. (1982) 'An Information System for the Social Casework Agency: a model and case study', *Administration in Social Work*, vol. 5, no. 3/4.

Powell, F. (1980) 'Is Big Brother Watching You?', *Social Work Today*, 24 June.

Rees, S. J. (1978) *Social Work Face to Face*, London, Arnold.

Rose, M. (1969) *Computers, Managers and Society*, Harmondsworth, Middx, Penguin Books.

Sainsbury, E. E. (1977) *The Personal Social Services*, London, Pitman.

Schoech, D. and Arangio, T. (1979) 'Computers in the Human Services', *Social Work*, 24, March.

Schoech, D. and Schkade, L. L. (1980) 'Computers Helping Caseworkers', *Child Welfare*, vol. 59, no. 9.

Schoech, D., Schkade, L. L. and Mayers, R. S. (1982) 'Strategies for Information System Development', *Administration in Social Work*, vol. 5, no. 3/4.

Seddon, M. (1983) 'Computers – the new I.T.!', *Probation Journal*, June.

Sharron, H. (1984) 'The Ghost in the Machine', *Social Work Today*, 31 January.

Smith, N. J., Parmar, G. and Paget, N. (1980) 'Computer Simulation and Social Work Education', *British Journal of Social Work*, vol. 10, no. 4.

Transler, G. B. (1960) *In Place of Parents*, London, Routledge & Kegan Paul.

Tutt, N. (1983) Report of a Speech to Age Concern Conference, in *Community Care*, 10 February.

Vickery, A. (1977) *Caseload Management*, London, National Institute for Social Work.

Ward, D. (1981) 'Hampshire Social Services Department On-line System', *BURISA Newsletter*, 48.

Whaley, C. (1983) 'Computers in a Local Social Services Office', unpublished.

Wilshire, S. E. (1976). *Computer-based Management Information System: a brief description*, Research Report No 9, Winchester, Hampshire County Social Services Department.

Index